ESSENTIAL
STENCILS

ESSENTIAL
STENCILS

Samantha Barbic &
Jeremy Clements

Watson-Guptill Publications • New York

First published in the United States in 1999 by
Watson-Guptill Publications
a division of BPI Communications, Inc.
1515 Broadway
New York, NY 10036

A QUARTO BOOK

Library of Congress Cataloging-in-Publication Data

Barbic, Samantha.
    Essential Stencils / Samantha Barbic and Jeremy Clements.
        p.   cm.
    Includes index.
    ISBN 0-8230-1623-4 (pbk.)
    1. Stencil work.   I. Clements, Jeremy.   II. Title.
TT270.B365   1999
746.6—dc21
                                    98-40660
                                    CIP

This book was designed and produced by
Quarto Publishing plc
The Old Brewery
6 Blundell Street
London N7 9BH

Art editor: Suzanne Metcalfe-Megginson
Designer: Alison Mayze
Illustrators: Jenny Dooge, Nicola Gregory, Pippa Howes, Kate Simunek
Photographer: Iain Bagwell, Colin Bowling
Picture researcher: Gill Metcalfe
Senior editor: Anna Watson
Copy editors: Alison Wormleighton, Hilary Sagar, Claire Waite
Publisher: Marion Hasson
Art Director: Moira Clinch
Assistant Art Director: Penny Cobb
QUAR.STE

Manufactured in China by Regent Publishing Services Ltd.
Printed in China by Leefung-Asco Printers Ltd.

BEFORE YOU START

STENCILING PROJECTS

CONTENTS

Stenciling is an enjoyable and easy way to decorate your home, requiring only basic skills and common sense to achieve great results. You can make wonderful, elaborate designs with a professional-looking finish, so only your imagination can hold you back.

INTRODUCTION

40 projects

Each of the ten design themes contains four projects, which have step-by-step instructions, grids and a photograph of the finished piece.

This book is designed to get you started straight away. You needn't worry about designing and cutting out stencils to start with, because we provide you with thirty original designs already cut for you to use. These stencils have been designed to complement each other so that you can create different decorative schemes by combining them in groups, using them individually, or choosing different color combinations.

By using these stencils you will learn the principles of design and decoration, and armed with this knowledge and practical experience, you will then be able to create your own designs with confidence. The book starts with some basic lessons about design and color use, followed by a section on the basic stenciling equipment and techniques needed to get you started.

The stenciling projects are arranged in ten sections, each with its own design theme. The context for the

Inspirations pages introduce each theme

Name of design theme

Explanatory text about the theme

Illustrations of art relating to the theme

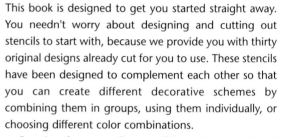

4

The ancient Greeks lived more than two thousand years ago, but the vocabulary of design which they developed, and which the Romans adapted, has dominated Western style ever since. When looking for ideas, classical ornamentation will provide much inspiration.

CLASSICAL *inspirations*

Although little is known about Greek interior decoration, many examples of painted pottery, engraved metalwork, and both painted and sculpted friezes have been excavated. Also, a number of Greek temples and palaces are still standing. Strict laws of proportion were applied throughout buildings, from the grand plan to the moldings. Architectural features such as columns with ornate capitals, and sculpted friezes on walls, were painted with natural pigments.

Red oxide, black, and ocher *are used in the decoration of this ancient Greek bowl.*

The Greeks had an overriding interest in proportion and pattern, in whatever scale or medium. Figurative work appeared in both decoration and art but although they were great observers of nature, they rarely tried to copy it directly. Typical ornament can be seen on the many earthenware vases that have been excavated. Patterns made of interlocking straight lines, known as frets or Greek keys, were combined in numerous ways.

Another form utilized by the Greeks was the scroll, which was used mainly as a linking device or stem for Greek floral ornament. It is difficult to identify particular flowers and plants within Greek decoration, as the motifs are stylized. Other Greek motifs include the acanthus leaf, vine leaf and grapes, palmette, ivy, and laurel.

We don't really know exactly what colors were used, as they have faded with time or been washed away by the elements. The sculpted white marble and alabaster of the temples that were once colorfully and intricately decorated. On the floors, however, many mosaics remain. Made of stone, clay, and glass, they contain rich colors, including oxide reds, azure blues, and golds.

Historic events and *legends were depicted in a decorative fashion on ancient vases.*

The Romans based their art forms on the Greek prototypes, elaborating on the scroll and creating ever more ornate and literal interpretations. A thousand years after the fall of the Roman Empire, the Renaissance in Europe marked a return to the classical vocabulary. Then, in the mid-18th century in Europe, and about 30 years later in America, the Neoclassical movement turned back to Greek and Roman models for inspiration. In Britain the architect Robert Adam created graceful adaptations of the Greek and Roman forms, and in America a similar approach prevailed in the Federal style of architecture.

As part of the eighteenth-century enthusiasm for all things classical, the proportions of rooms were determined by mathematical laws. To achieve ideal proportions, walls were divided into sections—coving, freeze, picture rail, infill or field, chair rail, dado, and baseboard—with the proportions of each section corresponding to those of the separate parts of a Greek column on a pedestal.

In modern houses, of course, these divisions have almost disappeared. For a contemporary interpretation of these sections, stenciled borders or dados are ideal and can be applied in either contrasting colors or different tones of the same color.

This building in Charleston, *America, shows the influence of Neoclassicism.*

Though the *original colors are gone, we can still find inspiration in the architectural forms of Greece, such as these sandy, weathered columns set against a vivid blue sky.*

Right: the three *classical orders; Corinthian, Doric, and Ionic.*

51

themes is either geographical or historical with patterns inspired by different cultures, or they relate to a particular subject such as the garden or a children's bedroom. The creative sources which inspired each theme are introduced with color photographs and illustrations and information about typical motifs and colors to use.

Following this there are two pages of examples of stencil and color combinations which can be created using the particular stencils chosen for that theme. There are four step-by-step projects in each theme, showing how you can decorate a variety of objects, ranging from walls and floors to furniture, accessories, and drapes. All the projects are shown together in a real room setting at the end of the theme.

The concluding section of the book is called Make Your Own Stencils, which uses step-by-step photographs to show you how to create stencils from your own designs. The purpose of the book as a whole is to introduce you to the delights of decorating your home with stencils and to encourage you to create new stencils in any style your imagination conjures up.

Combinations pages show more design options

Artworks showing extra central motifs, borders, and repeat patterns linked to each theme

Illustrations of additional projects you could make

Stencils used in the theme

Photograph of all the theme's projects in a real room setting

Project pages explain how to stencil your home

Project title

Step-by-step instructions

List of equipment needed

Stencils used

Project template

Photograph of finished project

BASIC
TECHNIQUES

Only a little equipment is needed for stenciling—the stencils used in the projects within this book are supplied pre-cut, and other items are shown below.

Pencils
For marking grids and repeats.

Masking tape
It is best to use low-tack decorator's tape.

Stencil brushes
A conventional stencil brush offloads paint from short, compact bristles. The stiff bristles are very durable and the brush should last a long time if looked after well.

Eraser

Pens
For drawing out designs and master stencils.

Paint brushes
Used for background painting, borders, and framing.

Oiled manila stencil card

Drawing paper

Tracing paper

Coarse-grade sandpaper

Fine-grade sandpaper

Plumb line
With chalk on the line, this is an excellent tool for marking out grids.

Tape measure

Craft knife or mat knife *For cutting master stencils.*

Scissors

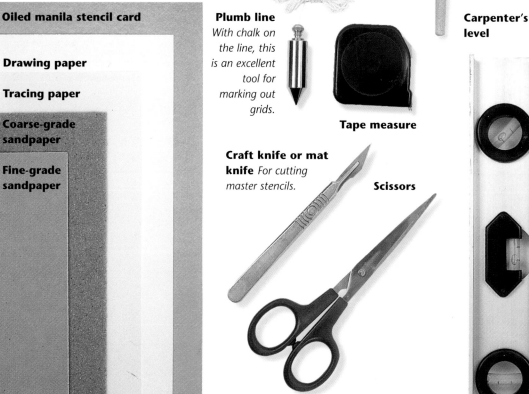

Carpenter's level

Yardstick

Using Grids

To stencil a repeating design, you will need to mark out a grid. This will help you position the stencils accurately, and will save you time in the long run. The grid is made up of perpendicular lines, either horizontally and vertically (forming squares) or diagonally (forming diamonds). Be sure to measure accurately when marking out the grid, and check when you are drawing the lines that they are exactly at right angles to each other (a carpenter's square or even a CD case or a book will help).

Marking out grids

1 For a grid of squares, mark points at the desired spacing along all four sides of the surface. They should be no farther apart than the length of your yardstick, so if necessary, mark intermediate points too. Using the yardstick, join the marks with straight lines.

2 For a grid of diamonds, mark out a large square area, and draw straight lines between diagonally opposite corners. Draw your grid lines parallel to these, the desired distance apart. Extend the lines beyond the square area as necessary to fill the entire surface.

Using a chalked plumb line

If you have a helper, a quick way of marking lines is with a chalked plumb line (or snap cord). Rub chalk over a plumb line or piece of string and hold it taught against the wall. Pull the string away from the wall and snap it back so that it leaves a chalk mark on the wall.

Registration lines

1 Registration lines marked on your stencil card are an easy way to align stencils on a grid. Draw a line through the center of the motif and out to the edge of the card mount. Do the same horizontally.

2 Align these marks against your grid. To center a stencil within the spaces of a grid, rather than on the lines, you need pairs of registration lines the same distance apart as the grid size. Mark them symmetrically either side of the motif.

Application Techniques

Once you have positioned your stencil as you want it, then you need to tape it in place with low-tack decorator's masking tape. If you do not tape it down there is a risk that it will slip while you are applying the paint, or that it will not lie flat and you will not get a sharp edge to the design.

Flat brush

A flat decorating brush can be used instead of a stenciling brush to apply an opaque layer of paint. It is effective for quickly applying a strong-colored ground as a base for a metallic color, such as deep vermilion under bronze. When using a flat brush, take care not to let the bristles get caught under the stencil edges.

Sponge

Sponges are useful for achieving various effects, from chainlike threads of color to blending two or more shades into a wash. Natural sponges tend to leave more pronounced marks than synthetic versions and are useful for producing faux stone effects. The imprint is a series of open spaces linked by an organic, threadlike structure.

Stencil brush

The standard method of applying paint with a stencil brush, sometimes known as pouncing, uses fast dabbing movements, almost like hammering with the brush. The pouncing action creates an even, softly stippled effect. Avoid too heavy an application of paint. The density of color can be increased if it is too light, but it can't be taken away, so just take up a tiny amount of paint onto a barely damp brush, and work the paint into the brush before stenciling.

Fabric

All manner of textured fabrics can be used to create interesting finishes. The weave on this particular cloth produces an attractive woolly effect.

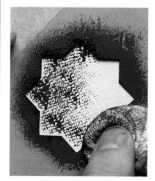

Banding and Framing

Sometimes a design appears to be unresolved or floating free, and what is needed may be to edge the design with some banding (stripes) or to contain it within a frame (in other words, bands that form a rectangle).

1 Use a yardstick to draw guidelines for the edges of the bands, keeping it horizontal with a carpenter's level. Run low-tack masking tape outside the lines. Press it down firmly or the paint might seep underneath.

2 Using a flat brush, paint between the masked lines until the band is the desired density of color.

3 Remove the masking tape by slowly and carefully pulling it back on itself. It is important to do this while the paint is still wet otherwise it may crack and give you an uneven finish.

4 When all the tape has been removed, you will have neat, straight lines. You can link horizontal lines together with pairs of vertical lines to create a frame shape.

Spray paint

Spray paint is useful when you are trying to cover a large area. Once you have taped the stencil in place, mask the rest of the area with card or newspaper to protect from overspray. You can create different effects with spray paint by varying the density of the spray. The other useful feature of spray paint is that two colors can be blended together with subtle variations.

Crumpled cloth

As well as stenciling with pieces of fabric of different textures, bunching a domestic dish cloth together into folds and pleats creates an interesting effect. The bunched-up dish cloth needs to be turned regularly in order to keep the texture fresh.

Spacing

For many projects involving repeated images, regular spacing is essential. To achieve this, first measure the width of the surface you are stenciling, whether it is a small object or the walls of a room. Divide this figure by the approximate width of one repeat (i.e. from the beginning of one set of motifs to the beginning of the adjacent one). If the result is not a whole number, round it up to the nearest whole number, and divide that number back into the total width. This new figure is the exact width of one repeat.

If you are stenciling a linear repeat pattern over a large area, you can save time by adding registration marks and a "spacer" to the stencils, as shown here.

1 Cut a "spacer" strip from stencil card or Mylar (clear acetate film). Tape this onto the side of the stencil so that the total width from the edge of the spacer to the far edge of the motif is exactly the same as your repeat. Pencil registration lines from the top and bottom of the motif across to the edge of the spacer.

2 Use the registration marks to line up the stencil with the previously stenciled motif, and align the left edge of the spacer with the right edge of that motif. Tape in place and then stencil. Repeat along the line.

3 To fill the spaces with another motif, you need to center it horizontally and vertically. Either cut the stencil to the same size as the space you want to fill, or draw registration lines.

4 Tape the stencil in place in the usual way, and stencil the motif. Repeat the process all along your object or wall.

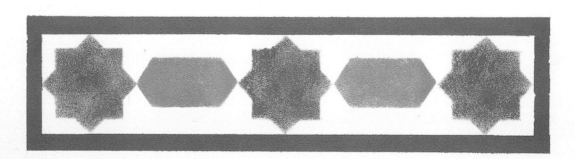

5 The dimensions of this frame were planned so that the eight-pointed stars and lozenges would fit neatly within it. Careful planning will give your designs a professional look.

Master Stencils

If you are stenciling a design containing lots of motifs that are repeated several times, it will probably be quicker for you to make a master stencil. Although it takes time to make, this will be offset by not having to position each motif individually, over and over.

1 Plan out the design on a piece of paper, starting at the center and working outward. Position the individual stencils and draw through them with a pencil. Transfer the design to the stencil card or to Mylar (clear acetate film). For card you have to trace or use carbon paper. For Mylar you can simply copy over the image using a fiber-tip pen.

2 Place the stencil on a cutting mat and use a sharp craft knife or mat knife to cut out each motif. Use one hand to hold the stencil still, keeping your hand well away from the blade and not in the line in which you will be cutting. Always cut toward yourself. Change direction by turning the stencil not the knife. Try to cut each curve with a single stroke.

Preparing Your Surfaces

You need a smooth, clean, grease-free surface on which to stencil. Spending a little time on preparation will ensure a good result every time.

1 Any smooth surface, such as varnished wood or metal, will need to be sanded with coarse-grade sandpaper. This allows the paints to grip on the surface.

2 Once you have sanded, dust off the surface and paint it with primer. Leave it to dry. You can then paint the object with latex (emulsion) paint in your chosen background color.

If you are painting on a wall that already has latex paint in the color you want, then it is a good idea to wash it down before stenciling, to ensure the surface is grease-free. Even slight traces of grease can repel the paint and will give you an uneven finish.

DESIGN INSPIRATIONS

The first stage of decoration is the ideas stage. An inspired idea for a stenciling project can come to you at any moment, though in fact your subconscious may have been mulling it over for some time. The source of inspiration is most often your immediate environment, particularly with regard to color and pattern, the two most important elements of design.

By learning to look—really look—at your environment, you will find a wealth of inspiration. Pattern is everywhere, and nature provides not only a vast color palette but also a multitude of lessons on combining colors. Also look at the man-made environment. For example, the motifs on your carpet could provide a starting point for a stencil pattern for your walls.

Inspiring shapes and patterns *Look for interesting shapes in the environment around you—both natural and man-made.*

Books and magazines are useful sources of inspiration. Keep anything with an interesting shape, or a color combination you like, in a scrapbook, perhaps arranged into categories. You might, for example, keep all the ideas involving reds together. You could even take them a stage further, preparing ideas boards for specific projects, similar to the color boards interior designers produce.

Books and articles about history, other cultures, or the decorative arts are invaluable. Many motifs have a long history, having been reinterpreted and stylized by successive generations and different civilizations. If you can experience the arts and crafts of other cultures firsthand, so much the better. On vacation (at home as well as abroad), in museums, and at galleries, record interesting ideas with a camera, sketches, and notes.

What makes design and decoration so exciting are the different moods and interpretations that are possible. Every culture and generation has developed its own expressions of creativity, which provide an infinite source of inspiration for today's stenciler.

Arranging shapes

Pattern is basically the arrangement of shapes. Motifs can be arranged in numerous ways—formal, geometric, linear, rhythmical, or completely random.

Most repeated patterns that cover large, flat areas are made up of individual elements contained within imaginary grids. The grid formation, be it squares or diamonds, allows elements to be contained within the grid spaces or aligned at the points where the grid lines intersect. The elements can be placed in each square or diamond, or in alternate ones, checkerboard-fashion.

A continuous pattern based on a grid must use elements that are sympathetic with this. For example, any motif based on a cross can be centered over the intersection of the grid lines so that the four points of the cross fall on these lines. Any non-directional motif, such as a flowerhead, can fit within the spaces of the grid.

Continuous running wave
By linking the palmette motifs with a curl that changes direction, this pattern is very dynamic.

Repeat pattern
Repeating in all directions, this continuous pattern can be extended to cover any surface area.

You can create continuous patterns using directional motifs. For instance, place a heart in each of four squares (arranged in two rows of two) so that they are pointing toward the central intersection of lines. This four-square group can then be repeated across the grid.

Long horizontal runs can be divided up in various ways, each with a different visual rhythm. A continuous running wave can be kept quite simple, as in the repetition of a curl. More elaborate examples add tendril-like offshoots to emphasize the directional qualities of a pattern. Vertical series designs produce a more static look.

Panels or friezes made up of a number of motifs are useful for decorating in self-contained sections. They are useful for dividing up wall space, such as underneath a chair rail. The elements are arranged across a center line within a designated area corresponding to the wall. They can fall on the center line, so it cuts through the center motif, or they can be mirrored on either side of the center line. A mixture of directional and static designs can be used to build up the complete panel.

Applying stencils to a round shape may seem daunting but the principles are the same. Find the center of the circle, and divide it into quarters with lines that intersect at right angles. You can then subdivide these with another pair of lines at right angles to each other, and so on. Each segment will hold one or more stenciled motifs.

When working on furniture or other three-dimensional objects, consider the areas where stenciling would be possible, and think about their shape or form. With fabric, take into account its fluid nature—a pattern for curtains will not be seen flat, so think about how it will hang.

The important thing is to keep ideas flowing. Experiment on different surfaces with different designs and colorways, so that you will be ready to spring into action when the next idea for a project comes along.

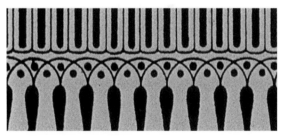

Vertical series design
A traditional way of arranging motifs, which gives a smart and formal look to any border.

Panel design
Working from a central line, panels of motifs can be built up using directional motifs and linking elements.

Background color

Plan your background color as carefully as the stencils themselves.

Color

Color is what brings most patterns alive. Even if you do not have a natural flair for choosing and combining colors, you can improve your skills by understanding how color works. Color is, in fact, light. Light rays vary in frequency, according to their position in the spectrum, which is why they are seen as different colors. When you look at a surface, the color you see is the light reflected from it. The pigment in every surface either absorbs or reflects light rays of particular frequencies, and so determines an object's color.

The mixing of paint is a "subtractive" process, which means that the more pigment, in the form of paint, you add to a surface, the more light the surface absorbs. This explains the muddied appearance that overmixing of paint often leads to. Paint colors are not, in fact, as pure as colored light—they contain small amounts of pigments that may be reflecting other colors.

Red, yellow, and blue are primary colors, which means they cannot be produced by mixing other colors. When two primaries are mixed, they produce a secondary color; red and yellow produce orange, red and blue produce violet, and yellow and blue produce green. A secondary color and the primary color that is *not* used to make it are described as being complementary. Blue and orange are complementary, as are yellow and violet, and red and green. When the primary and secondary colors are arranged in order of their frequencies (as in a rainbow—red, orange, yellow, green, blue, violet) around a circle, known as a color wheel, the complementary colors are opposite each other.

Adding a little of a paint color's complementary color to it is a useful way of reducing its intensity. If a color is used next to its complement, rather than being mixed with it, each will enhance the other. The complementary colors that are most often mixed or used together are those of the same value. A color's value indicates the amount of white/black, or light/dark, that has been added to it. Pink, for example, is red with white added, and the complementary color that is of the same value is mint green (i.e. green with white added).

Color samples

You can plan your designs most accurately if you refer to paint manufacturer's color samples.

Primary: Red

Secondary: Orange

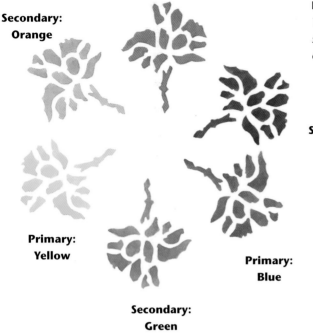

Primary: Yellow

Primary: Blue

Secondary: Green

Secondary: Violet

Primary and secondary color wheel

Two primary colors mixed together give a secondary color. Complementary colors are opposite each other.

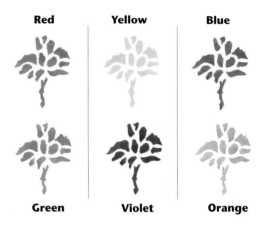

Red	Yellow	Blue
Green	Violet	Orange

Complementary colors

These color opposites need to be used carefully but are great for creating bright, vibrant designs.

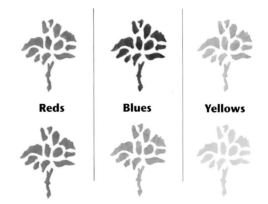

Reds	Blues	Yellows

Warm and cool colors

The colors in the top row are warm, and the bottom row cool. To avoid monotony in your decor, it is a good idea to add accents of cool color into a mainly warm color scheme, and vice versa.

Mixing a primary and a secondary color produces a tertiary color. These appear in between the primaries and secondaries in the spectrum and on a color wheel: red-orange, yellow-orange, yellow-green, blue-green, blue-violet, red-violet. The complements of tertiary colors are also tertiary, such as red-orange and blue-green.

The so-called earth colors, such as ochers, siennas, oxides, and umbers, which are made from natural pigments, produce subtle shades when added to other colors. You can create an interesting effect by using an earth color to reduce another color's intensity.

Colors can also be described as either warm or cool. Warm colors are red-violet, red, red-orange, orange, yellow-orange, and yellow; cool colors are yellow-green, green, blue-green, blue, blue-violet, and violet. Because of these color "temperatures," colors can have interesting optical effects on each other. For example, a warm color may suddenly look cooler when an even warmer one is placed next to it. Also, as a rule, warm colors appear to advance toward the eye more than cool colors, which seem to recede. This effect can be used in a stencil design by using the warmest color for the motif that is to be the focal point.

Ultimately, the most important thing to remember about color when stenciling is that using it should be fun. And the best way to learn how to use color, as well as pattern, is to experiment.

The stenciling projects in this book are divided into ten design themes, each of which uses the pre-cut stencils in different colors and patterns. Each theme starts with an introduction to its history and sources of inspiration for the contemporary stenciler. The subsequent two pages contain stencil patterns, color choices, and illustrations of objects for which you can adapt the patterns. Four step-by-step projects form the core of each theme, which are all shown together in a real-life setting as they might appear in your home. The last section of the book is called Make Your Own Stencils, which gives some suggestions of projects which you could make for yourself using hand-made stencils.

STENCILING PROJECTS

1

Informal and unpretentious, the country cottage is the epitome of rustic charm and coziness. For centuries, stenciling has been a popular way of decorating a cottage, using simple, small-scale motifs in keeping with its size ambience, and rural setting.

COUNTRY COTTAGE *inspirations*

A William Morris *print combining animal and plant motifs set within a lattice pattern.*

The appeal of the country cottage lies in its cheerful blending of the decorative and the functional. Natural materials and textures abound, and surfaces have the patina of age. An eclectic mix of furniture, chosen for its practicality and comfort, has accumulated over the years, producing an overall effect that is fresh and uncontrived.

Traditionally, cottage interiors have been inspired by the countryside surrounding them, and the stencil motifs used for the projects in this chapter—berries, the marguerite, the sprig, and the stalk and leafy stalk—are all based on nature.

Now that rural life has become, for many people, a means of escape from the city, the symbols of the countryside have become even more important. Images of meadows, flowers in bloom, trees, and birds singing evoke a time when life was slower and more in harmony with nature.

Many country cottages are decorated

Striking contrasts *of nature—vibrant magenta, lemon yellow, and lime green.*

with wallpapers bearing small prints of sprigs, rosebuds, or berries, and curtain fabrics with climbing geraniums, honeysuckle, or clematis. Cottage dwellers would stencil or paint freehand designs on their whitewashed walls, covering walls and wood framing as if one and the same. The aim was to create an effect similar to the expensive wallpapers and textiles used on the walls of wealthy homes in the cities. Similarly, floors were painted or stenciled in imitation of expensive imported rugs.

Today, of course, stenciled walls and floorboards are valued for their own artistic merit, but in the eighteenth and nineteenth centuries, paint was used for expediency. Not only did it provide colorful decoration at a fraction of the cost of handprinted wallpapers, but in those days it was the only means of protecting surfaces.

The wooden furniture found in cottages was painted too. Before the twentieth century, only fine-quality hardwoods were left unpainted; the softwood furniture that cottagers could afford would always have been painted. Today, both painted and unpainted wood furniture looks good in country cottages, and either type will benefit from stenciling.

Simple curtains in either muslin or other plain cotton fabrics are the most suitable for the country cottage look and are ideal for stenciling. Other textiles that could be stenciled include cushion covers, bed covers, pillowcases and shams, and tablecloths or placemats. Stenciled canvas floorcloths look wonderful in a rustic interior and are another traditional cottage furnishing with a long history.

You can also use stenciling to draw attention to architectural features in an old cottage, whether it is an attractive window frame, a mantelpiece, a sloping roof,

A floral print *combines soft natural colors set against a creamy background.*

The rose-covered *thatched cottage is an enduring image.*

or a narrow wooden staircase. Or use stenciling to create your own folk art, which is, of course, perfect for a cottage.

Just as country cottage motifs echo the countryside, so the colors of nature are the most suitable. As in nature, green makes an excellent foil for either subtle or strong colors. Its range and versatility are apparent if you think of apple green with russet, and vibrant lime green with delphinium blue.

Although you obviously will not want to change your color schemes with every season, decorating with a particular season in mind can produce successful, harmonious schemes. Moss green, cornflower blue, primrose yellow, and rose pink give a soft, airy, springlike look, or brick red, russet, gold, and ocher will produce a warm, cozy, autumnal effect. Cool stone white, forest green, and mulberry red could be used for a winter-inspired scheme, while buttercup yellow, lavender blue, apple green, and strawberry red all evoke summertime.

In a cottage garden the vivid *blue of a delphinium contrasts with vibrant green foliage.*

COUNTRY COTTAGE COMBINATIONS

Floral motifs, both literal and stylized, have been used in decorative work since ancient times. The versatile flowers, stem, and berry motifs shown here can be used in a variety of ways. For example, you can stencil formal grids and borders to complement a traditional English cottage interior or apply them in a random, abstract fashion to create a more contemporary look. Although any color is possible for these stencils, always consider the overall balance and the effect you want to create before making your color choice.

STENCILS

Marguerite

Stalk

Leafy stalk

Berries

Circle

Armchair cover
The repeat pattern, right, can be stenciled onto fabric, before you make a cover, or onto a readymade cover, following the panels and shape of the chair.

The marguerite and stalk motifs are used to create a bold, contemporary pattern that looks particularly good on fabric.

Bright colors add an extra dimension to this attractive design: the yellow and white circles draw the eye to the central flower, which is the main focus of the pattern.

White marguerites on a lemon yellow background are so bright and cheerful that they would brighten up any dark corner.

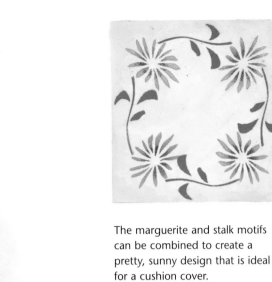

The marguerite and stalk motifs can be combined to create a pretty, sunny design that is ideal for a cushion cover.

Waste-paper basket
It is possible to stencil on surfaces that are not smooth for a very homely, textured effect.

Chest of drawers
To adapt the repeat pattern below, each drawer-front is treated as a separate panel.

This bright, contemporary repeat pattern is perfect for curtain fabric or a wallcovering.

Combine the leafy stalk and berry motifs to create a pattern with a mellow, autumnal feel.

FLOWERY CURTAINS

Take your inspiration from garden flowers and bring a light, summery look into your home; stencil flowers and leaves in fresh grassy green and sunny yellow onto readymade white muslin curtains. Or for a bolder look, dye the fabric yellow first and stencil the flowers in red, or dye it blue then stencil yellow flowers.

YOU WILL NEED

Readymade white muslin curtains

Sheet of plastic to protect work surface

Tape measure

Ruler

Pencil

Masking tape

Fabric paints: leaf green, cadmium yellow

Stencil brush

Iron

STENCILS

Marguerite   Stalk

POSITIONAL GUIDE

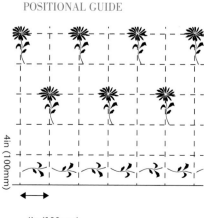

4in (100mm)

4in (100mm)

1 Lay the curtains on a large, flat surface, protected by a plastic sheet. For the border within the bottom hem, find the number of repeats by dividing the width of the fabric by the width of the repeat. Our stencil width when horizontal is 3¼in (85mm) and the spacing ¾in (20mm), giving a repeat of 4in (100mm). Inset the design from the edges if it does not fit perfectly.

2 Starting at the left edge of the hem, tape the stencil stalk motif horizontally in place and stencil in leaf green fabric paint. Once the paint is dry, turn the stencil over (still horizontal) and stencil ¾in (20mm) away from the first motif, using the bottom of the curtain as a guide to keep the design straight. Continue across the hem in this way, turning the stencil over each time.

3 The main pattern for the curtains is based on a grid, with the motif placed on alternate squares in a checkerboard pattern. We used a grid with 4in (100mm) squares, marking with faint pencil just the corner points of each square rather than drawing out the whole grid. A wider grid spacing would produce a light, airy feel, while reducing the grid size would create a denser pattern.

4 Stencil the flowers on each alternate point, using the marguerite stencil and the cadmium yellow fabric paint. For extra color interest stipple a little of the green paint over some of the flowers. Then stencil the green stems and leaves using the stalk stencil.

5 If the manufacturer's instructions require it, fix the fabric paint with an iron.

FLOWERY PILLOW COVER

Brighten up your bedroom with colorful pillows with pretty floral patterns. Plain pillow covers can be given a new lease on life with fabric dye and these decorative motifs. Use the three stencils in the arrangement shown here or combine them in different ways and toning colors on a group of pillows.

POSITIONAL GUIDE

1 Dye the cover in the washing machine, following the manufacturer's directions, then iron it. Protect your work surface with a plastic sheet. Measure your pillow cover to see how many leafy stalks will fit around the edge, insetting the design if necessary. We have used five along the length and four along the width.

2 Place the leafy end of the leafy stalk stencil in one corner, using the edge of the pillow cover to make sure it is straight; tape it down and stencil in pale green. When dry turn the stencil over, and place it with the ends touching and lined up with the first motif, so it is a mirror image of the first one; stencil. Continue in this way to the next corner, finishing with the leafy end in the corner.

3 Turn the stencil and place it with the leafy end next to the corner, leaving a small space. Continue all the way around the pillow until you reach the starting point.

4 With the marguerite stencil, stencil a flower in each corner, about 3½in (90mm) in from the border.

5 Stencil a marguerite flower in the center of the cover. About ⅜in (10mm) away from the flower, add the stem using the stalk stencil.

6 To make the cover washable, fix the paints with an iron following the manufacturer's directions.

YOU WILL NEED

White cotton pillow cover

Washing machine dye: leaf green

Iron

Sheet of plastic to protect work surface

Tape measure

Masking tape

Fabric paint: pale green

Stencil brush

STENCILS

Marguerite

Stalk

Leafy stalk

BERRY WALL PATTERN

This stenciling project gives you the best of both worlds: a decorative repeat pattern and the handmade look and attractive texture of paint. What's more, you have neither the expense of wallpaper nor its noticeable seams. Marking out the grid accurately is rather laborious but well worth the effort.

YOU WILL NEED

Latex paint: pastel green

Decorator's brush

Steel tape measure or yardstick

Pencil

Snap cord

Masking tape

Stencil paint: leaf green

Stencil brush

Eraser

STENCIL

Berries

POSITIONAL GUIDE

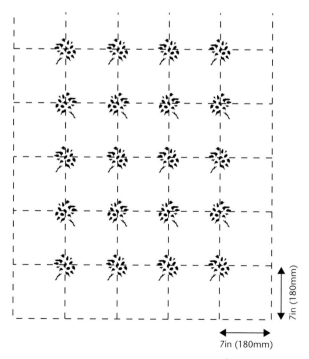

7in (180mm)

7in (180mm)

1 Begin by painting the walls with two coats of pastel green latex paint. Leave it to dry after each coat. Next, lightly draw a grid on the walls. The squares should be about 7in (180mm) across, but the exact size depends on the distance around your walls. Divide that distance by 7in (180mm). Round the amount off to the nearest whole number and then divide that back into the total distance. The resulting figure is the size of the squares in your grid that will fit around your room exactly.

2 Start at the top of the wall, about 2in (50mm) in from the corner, and use a pencil to mark the first vertical row of grid points. Next mark the top row (along the ceiling) and the bottom row (along the baseboard). At the other corner of the wall, mark the last vertical row for that wall, in line with the last mark in the top row. Now get someone to help you mark out the grid using a chalked plumb line.

3 Continue the process on the remaining walls, measuring from the last vertical line on the wall you have just done and marking the grid on each wall before you start the next one. When you get back to the first corner, the grid should meet perfectly.

4 Begin in one corner at the bottom of the grid, placing the berry stencil on the bottom line and centering it on a cross in the grid; tape in place and stencil. Repeat on each cross along this line all the way around the room.

5 Move up to the next line and stencil in the same way but with the stencil turned over (the flowers should still be at the top). Move up the walls, alternating the direction of the stencil for each row.

6 Once the paint is dry, you can rub out any traces of the pencil grid with an eraser. Any chalk marks from the chalked plumb line can be wiped off.

BERRY PEG BOARD

Sometimes the most important thing about stenciling is working out the way to fit your stencils within the shape of the object you want to decorate. Often, it is best to keep your design simple rather than producing something which looks cluttered or fussy. This peg board design uses only one stencil, but it is carefully positioned to give an elegant result.

1 Prepare the surface of the wood by sanding and priming it (see Basic Techniques). Using the flat brush, paint two coats of pale yellow latex paint over the whole board, leaving it to dry completely after each coat.

2 With the tape measure, measure the gap between the pegs and work out the halfway point. Mark this point with a pencil and then draw a vertical line extending from the point to the top and bottom edges of the board.

3 On the berry stencil, mark a vertical line through the visual center of the stencil, to act as a registration line. Place the stencil on the board aligning both pencil lines so that it sits at the same height as the pegs. Tape in position and stencil lightly in olive green.

4 Repeat the measuring and marking at the halfway point between the next two pegs, and continue stenciling along the whole peg board in the same way.

5 When the paint is dry, erase the pencil marks. With the varnishing brush apply a coat of flat acrylic varnish to protect the surface.

YOU WILL NEED

Plain wooden peg board

Latex paint: pale yellow

2in (50mm) flat brush

Steel tape measure

Pencil

Masking tape

Stencil paint: olive green

Stencil brush

Eraser

Flat acrylic varnish

Vanishing brush

STENCILS

Berries

POSITIONAL GUIDE

2

The medieval period, or Middle Ages, lasted about a thousand years and later inspired both the "Gothick" style of the 18th century and the 19th-century Gothic revival. As a result, many medieval designs are still available and are as inspiring and versatile today as they ever were.

MEDIEVAL *inspirations*

Elaborate decoration *was applied to manuscripts, as seen on this capital.*

The Church dominated the arts and architecture of the Middle Ages. It was a time of Christian conquests throughout the world, and the Crusades against the Moors caught the imagination of Christian Europe, resulting in some of the greatest art of the Middle Ages. Today, the best place to find inspiration for motifs from this period is in Europe's medieval churches, cathedrals, and monasteries. Remnants of decoration can be seen in their carved paneling, altar decorations, and textiles. Traces of warm, earth colors remain on the walls; they have faded through the centuries, but once they would have been very bright, because raw pigments like ocher, sienna, terra verde, and ultramarine were used. One can get a better idea of the effect of these vibrant colors from stained-glass church windows, as much medieval stained glass remains intact. Illuminated manuscripts are also a vital source of inspiration.

Medieval interiors varied according to the wealth of the occupant, though even the grandest house would seem spartan by today's standards. Cold stone floors and drafty, dimly-lit rooms were the lot of everyone. Cottages had virtually no decoration apart from simple wall decoration painted or stenciled by the occupants using earth colors. Often the whitewashed plaster was simply painted with red lines in imitation of masonry, or with geometric motifs, crude ecclesiastical motifs, or rustic

A 15th-century tapestry with *beautifully faded reds, blues, and ochers.*

images, such as fruits, vegetables, or flowers.

Grander houses were painted in a relatively simple way, but also had furnishings, wall hangings, tapestries, and pillows. As well as providing decoration, these kept the warmth in and reduced drafts. They were also portable, which was essential since royalty and the nobility spent their lives moving between their various houses. The rich patterns combined with the warm tones of wood paneling provided a contrast to the austerity of the building. Furniture, usually made of dark hardwoods, was heavy, solid, and unupholstered. The only light came from candles, creating a dark and moody atmosphere.

Fabrics combined geometric patterns and motifs such as diamonds, squares, and rectangles with floral motifs like the fleur-de-lis. Originally based on the lily (the name is French for "flower of the lily"), this is a small heraldic device that was the former royal arms of France.

Heraldic motifs were increasingly used in homes toward the end of the Middle Ages. Coats of arms and crests were signs of a family's power, and they were also decorative and attractive in repeat patterns, so they were painted on walls, woven into textiles, and incorporated in

Encaustic tile designs
would be used as repeat patterns for a floor.

silver and stained glass.

In the eighteenth century, so-called "Gothick" houses used some Gothic architectural motifs, such as ogee arches and quatrefoils. Many of the medieval designs were copied more seriously and carefully by the Victorians during the Gothic revival that swept Europe and the United States. Because they were reproduced on fabrics and wallpapers, many original designs are still available today, along with new designs based on a medieval theme.

The bold geometric shapes of these motifs, such as crowns, crosses, stars, and fleurs-de-lis, produce wonderful patterns that can be stenciled onto any surface. Rooms can be divided with curtains stenciled with repeated floral patterns which could be echoed on pillows or wall hangings. Small motifs such as the fleur-de-lis work well on vases and containers. The stencils used in this chapter, including the cross, medieval leaf spray, and fleur-de-lis, offer great scope in all these areas.

A fine illuminated
page from a medieval manuscript, showing a royal banquet.

MEDIEVAL COMBINATIONS

The medieval motifs are extremely flexible and can be combined to form spectacular grid patterns for walls, floors, and furniture; linear borders; and individual emblems. The motifs can be used on large, flat surfaces as well as small, detailed objects. You can create dynamic emblems by combining motifs such as the solid diamond, solid heart, and the spikey medieval leaf sprays and by using several colors. Try using contrasting colors such as blue and ocher to add extra interest to grid combinations.

STENCILS

Cross

Heart

Fleur-de-lis

Diamond

Medieval leaf spray

A rich, well-balanced pattern is created with blue medieval leaf-spray stencils on a vivid background of gray-blue and warm ocher diamonds.

A combination of the cross and fleur-de-lis motifs makes a striking design that interlocks to give a strong repeat pattern.

A bold, powerful pattern is created by repeating the heart and fleur-de-lis motifs in red and green.

Pitcher

For a metal pitcher you will need to use special enamel paints to get a durable finish. Ceramics can be painted with acrylic paints, but they will not be dishwasher-safe.

Floor pattern

A richly-colored variation of the pattern on the right could transform dull cork tiles and brighten up your kitchen.

This elegant design in rich colors can stand on its own in a panel or can be repeated to form a striking pattern.

The rich colors and dynamic combination of cross and outward pointing fleur-de-lis motifs evoke images of a medieval battle with shields and flying arrrows. This design can be used alone or repeated on a diagonal grid.

Floor border

If you want a more sparing use of stencils in your home, make up a border one or two panels deep based on the motif on the left.

A somber effect is created by stenciling the motifs in gray, white, and ocher on a deep green background.

CROSS AND HEART TILES

Take inspiration from the encaustic tiles of the Middle Ages and use warm earth colors to create a decorative backsplash (or an entire wall) for your kitchen. Tiles are perfect for stenciling as there is already a grid laid out so half the work is done for you. Endless patterns can be created with these two simple motifs.

POSITIONAL GUIDE

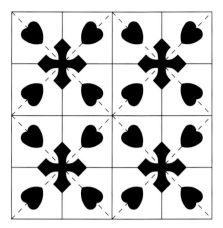

YOU WILL NEED

Tiles (in position)

2in (50mm) flat brush

Tile paints: ivory (optional—for base coat), brick red

Chalk

Ruler

Masking tape

Stencil brush

Cloth

* Tiles have a nonstick surface, so special paints have to be used to be durable. Tile paint, which is available in most home centers, comes in a range of colors, and is applied in the same way as ordinary paint.

STENCILS

Cross

Heart

1 Unless your tiles are already the color you want, use the flat brush to apply an ivory base coat and let dry. Start with four tiles forming a square at one bottom corner of the backsplash. Using chalk and a ruler, draw diagonal lines across the four tiles.

2 Draw diagonal lines on any four-tile squares alongside and above in the same way. For any row where there is only one tile left over, rather than two, just draw a line along the diagonal of the individual tile from corner to corner, as though the line were continuing onto another tile.

3 Stencil a cross in brick red where the two lines cross in the center of each four-tile square, lining up the four points of the stencil with the edges of the tiles and taping it in place while you stencil. At the edges, if there are only one or two tiles, use a quarter or a half of the stencil.

4 Stencil a brick red heart exactly halfway along the diagonal line on each tile. The bottom of the heart should point toward the cross. When the paint is dry, remove the chalk marks with a cloth.

Brighten up your kitchen with FLEUR-
terra-cotta containers stenciled DE-LIS
with different decorative motifs; STORAGE
choose either the
cream, yellow, and STORAGE
blue we have used here or colors that go
with your kitchen color scheme. These POTS
pots are quite small, so simple motifs are better; larger containers,
however, could have quite complex patterns and borders.

1 Wrap a piece of string around the pot and cut it at the point where the ends meet. Measure the length of the string to find the circumference of the pot. From this you can work out how many repeats will fit onto the pot (see Basic Techniques). Using the pencil, mark your repeat distances on the string.

2 Wrap the string around the pot, halfway up. Use the pencil mark on the pot where the repeat marks on the string come. Draw a vertical line through each of these points.

3 Place the medieval leaf spray with the vertical lines on the pot going through the top point and the center of the bottom of the motif, so that it is centered vertically. Tape the stencil firmly in place so that it is flat against the curved surface. Stencil in Prussian blue.

4 Measure 2in (50mm) from each side of the vertical line, and draw vertical lines through these points. Center the fleur-de-lis on these lines with the bottom edge even with that of the leaf spray. Tape in place and stencil in Prussian blue. Repeat on the other side.

5 For a second, complementary pot, use the heart stencil in cream and then stencil a fleur-de-lis in yellow over the center of the heart. The fleur-de-lis is repeated in yellow 2in (50mm) either side of the central motif but should align with the bottom of the central fleur-de-lis rather than the bottom of the heart.

6 When the paint is dry, erase the pencil lines. You can create many variations of these patterns, or just use plain hearts or a plain fleur-de-lis on other pots, depending on how many you want to decorate.

YOU WILL NEED

Terra-cotta pots

String

Ruler

Pencil

Masking tape

Stencil paints: Prussian blue, cream, yellow

Stencil brush

Eraser

STENCILS

Heart

Fleur-de-lis

Medieval leaf spray

POSITIONAL GUIDES

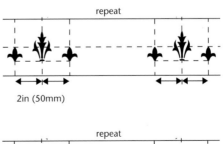

2in (50mm)

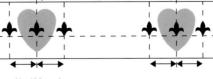

2in (50mm)

MEDIEVAL KITCHEN CABINETS

The fleur-de-lis and diamond, typical medieval motifs, can be used to make a strong geometric pattern that is ideal for flat surfaces. Different colors will create different effects—try a bold and a neutral color for the diamonds, as here, or two bold shades, or two neutrals with colorful fleurs-de-lis.

POSITIONAL GUIDE

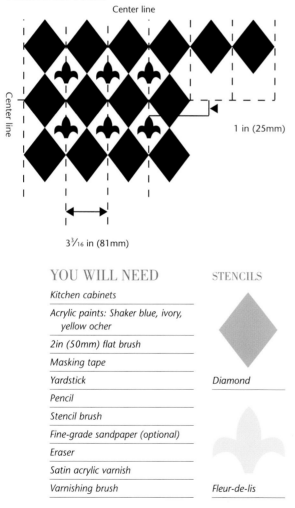

Center line

Center line

1 in (25mm)

3³⁄₁₆ in (81mm)

YOU WILL NEED

Kitchen cabinets

Acrylic paints: Shaker blue, ivory, yellow ocher

2in (50mm) flat brush

Masking tape

Yardstick

Pencil

Stencil brush

Fine-grade sandpaper (optional)

Eraser

Satin acrylic varnish

Varnishing brush

STENCILS

Diamond

Fleur-de-lis

1 It is easier to paint kitchen cabinet doors if you remove them from the hinges and lay them out flat, but it is not essential. Prepare the surfaces (see Basic Techniques) then paint the outer frame of each door with two or three coats of Shaker blue paint, using the flat brush. To get a clean, straight line, you may find it easier to mask the inner panel with tape; if so, remove the tape immediately afterward.

2 When this has dried, paint the inner panel with ivory, again masking the edge if necessary and removing the tape before the paint dries. If your doors have a completely flat surface, rather than panels, you can create a panel any size you like just by painting it.

3 Measure the length of the inner panel and the length of the diamond motif, and work out how many times the diamonds will fit into the panel. There will be no spacing between the diamonds, so you will probably need to have partial diamonds at top and bottom. This does not matter, so long as they are centered.

4 Lightly mark with a pencil the horizontal and vertical central lines of the panel. Mark a series of parallel vertical lines on either side of the central line. The spaces between the lines should be exactly 3³/₁₆ in (81mm) apart—this is the width of the diamond stencil.

5 Line up the right-hand point of the diamond stencil with the center point of the panel. Tape it down securely and then stencil in Shaker blue.

6 Position the stencil to the right of the central vertical line, lining it up as before, and stencil again. Move the stencil up to the diamond above this, line it up in the same way, and stencil. Continue systematically up and down the panel. Our cabinet doors had recessed sections around the central panels, so the stencil had to be creased into the recess to continue the pattern as though it was a flat surface. You may find that masking off the sides before you place the stencil will help you get a clean line at the edge.

7 Once the paint has dried, you can, if you wish, lightly sand the whole panel to give it a rough, aged look.

8 Draw a line down the length of the fleur-de-lis stencil going through the top point and the center of the base. Place the stencil on one of the central ivory diamonds, so the line goes through the top and bottom points of the diamond. The top of the fleur-de-lis should be about 1in (25mm) below the top of the diamond. Stencil in yellow ocher.

9 Continue stenciling fleurs-de-lis in each of the ivory diamonds in the central column. Run masking tape along the outside edge of the columns of partial ivory diamonds, and stencil partial fleurs-de-lis in these. Remove the tape immediately, pulling it back on itself very gently to avoid lifting the paint. When the paint is dry, you can, if desired, lightly sand the motifs.

10 Erase any visible pencil lines. Apply two coats of varnish so that the doors are protected and can be wiped clean easily.

HEART AND LEAF TRAY

Transform a plain wooden tray into a decorative feature which is both practical and elegant. We have used quiet earth tones to create a handpainted, rustic feel. However, if you want to achieve a more dramatic look, terra-cotta and yellow ocher against a background of blue-gray would look equally effective.

YOU WILL NEED

Painted or unpainted tray

Fine-grade sandpaper

Latex paint: ivory

2in (50mm) flat brush

Ruler

Pencil

Stencil paint: raw umber

Stencil brush

Masking tape

Eraser

Clear acrylic or polyurethane varnish

Varnishing brush

STENCILS

Medieval leaf spray

Heart

POSITIONAL GUIDE

1 Unless the tray is already painted, apply a base coat of ivory latex using the flat brush. If the tray is varnished you will need to sand it down before painting, otherwise the latex paint will not hold properly. Measure out and draw a pencil line midway along the length and another midway along the width of the tray—where they intersect is the center point.

2 Now draw two diagonal lines through the center cross at an angle of 45 degrees to the vertical. You will now have eight lines radiating out from the center.

3 Lay the stencils on the tray to see how they will fit. On our tray the medieval leaf spray motifs are 1¼in (30mm) from the center, and the hearts are 2in (50mm) from the center. Adjust the spacing to fit your tray.

4 Stencil a medieval leaf spray in raw umber on each of the horizontal and vertical lines.

5 Stencil a heart in raw umber on each of the diagonal lines, so it points to the center. The line should go through the point of the heart and, at the other end, through the indent of the two curves.

6 When the paint is dry remove the pencil marks with an eraser and then give the whole tray a light rub with sandpaper; this will bring out the texture of the wood grain and give the colors a softer look. Finally, varnish the tray to protect it from scratches and spills.

3

Moorish ornament is made up of boldly-colored geometric shapes in intricate patterns arranged on grids. Decoration is applied to every surface, but the motifs work best on flat surfaces. The overall effect is one of balance and harmony—an image of sophisticated refinement.

MOORISH *inspirations*

The Moors were a Muslim people of mixed Berber and Arab descent who hailed from northwest Africa. As Muslims they were forbidden to make any representations of Allah or human forms. As a result, the underlying structure of Moorish ornament is based on fixed principles founded on observations of geometry and natural forms.

The basis is a grid system, of which there are two versions: one in which every square is crossed by diagonal lines, and one in which the diagonal lines cross only alternate squares. The patterns that can be produced from these two grids is infinite. Curved elements are also added, making the design even more pleasing. However irregular the space to be decorated, the grid is always used to divide it.

The Generalife, *part of the Alhambra palace complex.*

After the form has been subdivided by the grid, the interstices are filled with ornament, which is then subdivided and enriched even more. Ornament is always used to decorate the structure of an object, from intricate carvings on a building to the fine metalwork on a chest.

The harmony of forms relies upon the balance and tension between the formal and fluid elements, each line forming from another, flowing gently, so that if any line or color were removed, the design would not work. It is a

A tile pattern using *the eight-pointed star, which was commonly used in Moorish design.*

similar process to tracing the veins of a leaf to a stem, then a branch, and finally to a root.

The Moorish use of color also involves rigid principles. To enhance the structural features of the building or object being decorated, colors are divided into categories: primary (red, yellow-gold, blue), secondary (purple, green, orange), and tertiary (mixtures of the primary and secondary colors). Nature is represented in the colors without being literally portrayed, since in nature blue and yellow-gold represent the sky and sun, while green symbolizes the trees and fields.

The most perfect example of Moorish decoration and architecture is the Alhambra, the ancient palace of the Moorish kings. The courtyards and dwelling rooms are composed of red brick and yellow sandstone with slender columns supporting horseshoe arches covered with rich ornamentation. The gardens are as remarkable as the palace itself, containing waterfalls, fountains, scented plants, and mosaic paving, all elaborately ornamented.

As a result of the highly influential nineteenth-century designer Owen Jones' publishing plans, elevations, and other details of the Alhambra, Moorish style became fashionable throughout the Victorian era. It was

In the Alhambra every detail of decorative *pattern serves to enhance the architectural features.*

characterized by this flat-patterned, rich surface ornament in geometric, floral, and calligraphic forms, while the architectural features included horseshoe and pointed arches; slender columns, often grouped; turrets and minarets; and bulbous or onion domes. Wealthy homes were often decorated in Moorish style, and "Turkish corners" were furnished with Ottoman velvets, prayer rugs, and Turkish kilims covering day beds, ottomans, window seats, and pillows.

Moorish style offers enormous scope to the stenciler. Floors, walls, ceilings, tabletops, chair backs, floorcloths, and other flat surfaces are ideal for this type of intricate, grid-based decoration. Typical motifs are those used for the stencils in this chapter—the lozenge, square, and five- and eight-pointed stars—which can be combined to create any number of colorful patterns.

Interlocking lozenges make up *this tiled wall in a typical Islamic style.*

MOORISH COMBINATIONS

Moorish design features highly complex and visually exciting geometric patterns. The key to creating these dynamic patterns is the repetition of one basic motif. Although only one motif is used, other eye-catching shapes are formed in the negative spaces between the repeated motifs. You can use color to draw attention to particular elements of the pattern. For example, motifs stenciled in a subtle color over a strong background will tend to recede and the eye will be drawn to the shapes created in the negative spaces. Try experimenting with bright colors to create exciting optical effects.

STENCILS

Eight-pointed star

Lozenge

Square

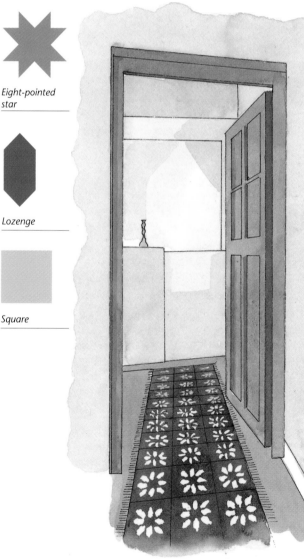

Lozenges can be combined to make a star shape that can be used on its own or repeated as a grid or border.

Runner

A plain canvas runner in your hall can be lightened by adding the lozenge pattern, above right. Fix your fabric dyes to ensure they are washable.

Repeating the lozenge motif diagonally creates a strong pattern with squares forming in the negative spaces.

Using the same color in different strengths brings harmony to the motifs and their background; repeating the pattern creates a lattice-like effect.

This pattern can be used as the centerpiece for a table or repeated to make a border. The eye is drawn to the deep red central star despite the bright lozenges surrounding it.

Wall hanging

Inspired by the rich wall patterns of the tiling in the Alhambra palace, the pattern at top right can be used to decorate your own wall hangings.

Using a deep blue for the star motifs focuses the eye on the stars and makes the squares and lozenges in the negative spaces recede into the background.

Wooden planter

The star pattern, left, can also be adapted for paneled items, although this places less emphasis on the optical effects of the negative spaces.

Complex patterns can be created simply be repeating one single motif; you can add further colors to achieve greater depth.

GEOMETRIC TABLETOP

Create an exotic table fit for the bazaars and tearooms of North Africa. For an opulent atmosphere, combine the table with low-level seating in the form of ornate rugs and rich, sumptuous pillows. Any number of geometric patterns can be created using different arrangements of these three simple motifs, and this design can be adapted for any shape of tabletop.

YOU WILL NEED

Coffee table (rectangular, square, or round)

Latex paint: ivory

2in (50mm) flat brush

Ruler

Pencil

Masking tape

Stencil paints: lapis blue, deep turquoise

Stencil brush

Eraser

Acrylic or polyurethane varnish

Varnishing brush

STENCILS

Eight-pointed star

Lozenge

POSITIONAL GUIDE

1 Prepare the coffee table surface (see Basic techniques) and paint it with ivory latex paint. When dry, draw lines in pencil halfway across the width and length of the tabletop. Place the eight-pointed star stencil at the point where the two lines cross, so that the drawn lines go through the centers of the small "V"s between the points of the star, and tape down the stencil.

2 Stencil the star in lapis blue and deep turquoise. Part of the charm of this piece is the textured effect of the paint within each stencil shape. This is achieved with a stencil brush by mixing the two colors together as you paint. Do not try to paint a solid color. Paint around the edges of the star stencil quite thickly, so that the outline of the shape will be clear. Then paint in the center of the shape more loosely, to give a mottled effect.

3 When the paint is dry, use a ruler to draw diagonal lines between the four larger "V"s, through the center point. You should now have eight lines radiating out from the center point. Measure out and mark along these lines where the stencils will be positioned, making the spaces between each stencil the same for all eight lines. On a circular table all the lines will have the same number of stencils; on rectangular or square tables the diagonal lines will have room for more stencils. On straight-edged tables allow extra space for a border around the edge.

4 Pencil in the border around the edge, and run masking tape outside the lines (see Basic Techniques). Apply lapis blue paint with a flat brush, then immediately remove the tape. If you don't remove the tape when the paint is wet there is a risk that the paint may crack and not give you a clean line.

5 Place the lozenge stencil so that one end point is at the first mark on one line and the line goes through the other end point as well. Tape it down and stencil in deep turquoise with lapis blue, mixing the two colors together as before. This time use more turquoise in the mixture, to give a lighter color overall. Repeat the lozenge shape in the same way on the other seven lines.

6 Next, place the star stencil on the second mark along one of the lines, with the line going through two of the larger "V"s. Stencil in the same colors and style as before. Repeat for the other seven lines. Continue working outward in this way, alternating lozenges and stars, until the tabletop is filled.

7 When the paint is dry, erase the pencil marks and varnish the whole table.

Geometric tabletop in turquoise: an alternative colorway is shown on page 49.

GOLDEN STAR WALL PATTERN

Bring formal harmony to your walls with a repeating design of simple shapes. This design combines the square stencil with the lozenge in an intricate decorative effect, to create the ornate geometric patterns of the Moors. It looks particularly effective combined with the border opposite.

YOU WILL NEED

Latex paint: ivory

Decorator's brush

Steel tape measure

Pencil

Yardstick

Snap cord (optional)

Masking tape

Stencil paints: wine red, gold

Stencil brush

Eraser

1in (25mm) flat brush (optional)

Fine-grade sandpaper (optional)

Flat acrylic varnish (optional)

Varnishing brush

1 Paint your wall with a base coat of ivory latex. You may need two coats, leave to dry between coats.

2 Mark the center point of the wall's width and from this point, mark out 6⁷⁄₈in (175mm) intervals across the wall. Also mark five intervals of this size vertically from the baseboard upward to a height of 34³⁄₈in (870mm).

3 Using a yardstick (or, if there are two of you, a chalked plumb line), connect these points diagonally to form a diamond-patterned grid. If the scale does not finish perfectly in the corner of the room, allow for a border (see opposite) on each side, and also along the top and bottom of the design.

4 Place one end point of the lozenge stencil in one corner of the bottom central diamond of the grid, and tape it down. Stencil using wine red paint. Dab the color on gently to give a textured finish. Repeat for the other corners of the diamond, so that the lozenge shapes overlap to form a cross. Continue up the row.

5 Stencil the next row of diamonds, where the points meet the ones you have just done; the row of diamonds in between should be left empty. Eight-pointed stars will appear in the negative (unstenciled) spaces. Continue working across the whole wall.

6 In the negative spaces, draw lines joining the corners of the diamonds, to form a cross at the center point. Center the square stencil over this point, aligning the corners with the lines of the cross to make a diamond; stencil with wine red. Fill all the negative spaces in this way. Now center the square stencil over each already stenciled square, turning the stencil 45 degrees to form an eight-pointed star; stencil in

STENCILS

Lozenge   Square

POSITIONAL GUIDE

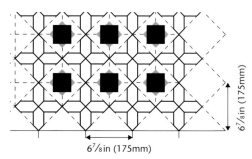

6⁷⁄₈in (175mm)

6⁷⁄₈in (175mm)

wine red. If you feel confident enough to cut your own stencils (see Basic Techniques) you could make a single star stencil for this step. Leave the paint to dry.

7 Repeat step 6 but paint a coat of gold over the wine red for a glowing effect. Erase the pencil lines.

8 Stencil a border around the edges, if desired (see next project), or just create a straight-line border (see Basic Techniques). For a slightly aged effect, rub it lightly with fine-grade sandpaper. Coat with flat acrylic varnish.

This ornate border would look good on its own, or you could combine it with the wall design opposite. The same stencils, colors, and equipment are used as for that project.

GOLDEN STAR BORDER

1 This wall border is designed to be at the height of a chair rail, which is normally about a third of the way up a wall. Mark the height all the way around the walls. Now mark another line, ¼in (5mm) above the first. Run masking tape outside these lines.

2 Mark another line, 4in (100mm) up from the bottom of the upper tape, and mark one more line ¼in (6mm) above that. Mask outside these lines as before. Using the flat brush, apply wine red paint between the upper pair of tape lines and again between the lower pairs of tape lines. Remove the tape before the paint is dry.

3 The stencils are 2¾in (70mm) wide and we used 1¼in (30mm) spacing between them, making the repeat 8in (200mm). Measure around the room and divide the measurement by 8in (200mm); if the stencil does not fit perfectly, adjust the spacing (see Basic Techniques). Mark the pattern repeats all the way around the room, halfway between the painted stripes.

4 Mark registrations line across the diagonal of the square stencil. Placing these registration marks on the pencil marks on the wall, stencil the square, placed diagonally, and lozenge alternately around the room in wine red. At the corners of the room, fold the stencils to avoid having to interrupt the pattern. Then go back over the square with another square turned by 45 degrees to give a star shape.

5 Once the wine red paint has dried, the star shapes will need a further coat of gold. For a time-worn look, rub the paintwork back with sandpaper when dry. Varnish if desired.

POSITIONAL GUIDE

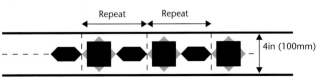

CUT-OUT LANTERN

Moorish lanterns have cutouts and colored glass to project intricate shapes and colors. This effect can be easily replicated by cutting shapes in cardboard. The patterns of the lantern give off a soft, atmospheric light.

YOU WILL NEED

17 x 22in (430 x 560mm) piece of manila cardboard

Yardstick

Pencil

Cutting mat

Craft knife or mat knife

Large sheet of red cellophane

Spray adhesive

White craft glue

* The cardboard used here is a standard size available from art supply stores, but you may need to use a different size or shape, depending on the size of the light or lamp you will be covering.

STENCILS

Square

Eight-pointed star

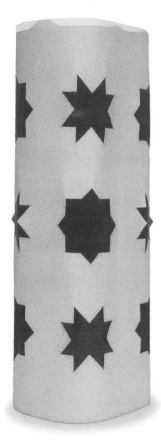

POSITIONAL GUIDE

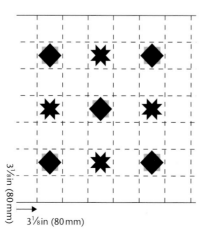

3⅛in (80mm)

3⅛in (80mm)

1 Create a new star shape from the square stencil by drawing one square, then turning it by 45 degrees and drawing another. Make a master stencil for this star shape (see Basic Techniques).

2 On the cardboard lightly pencil a grid of 3⅛in (80mm) squares—there will be an unused 1⅜in- (35mm-) wide strip along one long edge. Use the two star stencils to draw stars in alternate squares, alternating the two shapes, checkerboard fashion.

3 On a cutting mat, cut off the unused strip of cardboard along the long edge. Lightly score the shapes using a craft knife or mat knife, and then go back over the scored outline to cut them out. Cut toward you, taking care never to place the fingers of your other hand in line with the blade. Either paint the cardboard or leave it bare.

4 Spray the card with adhesive (such as the type used for mounting photographs) and lay the red cellophane over it. Press it down firmly all over and trim away any excess from around the edges.

5 Score the cardboard in three places to make a triangle, or roll it into a cylinder. Glue the overlapping edges at the back with white craft glue. Place the shade over a candle or a hurricane lamp, making sure it is not touching it anywhere.

4

The ancient Greeks lived more than two thousand years ago, but the vocabulary of design which they developed, and which the Romans adapted, has dominated Western style ever since. When looking for ideas, classical ornamention will provide much inspiration.

CLASSICAL
inspirations

Although little is known about Greek interior decoration, many examples of painted pottery, engraved metalwork, and both painted and sculpted friezes have been excavated. Also, a number of Greek temples and palaces are still standing. Strict laws of proportion were applied throughout buildings, from the grand plan to the moldings. Architectural features such as columns with ornate capitals, and sculpted friezes on walls, were painted with natural pigments.

Red oxide, black, and ocher
are used in the decoration of this ancient Greek bowl.

The Greeks had an overriding interest in proportion and pattern, in whatever scale or medium. Figurative work appeared in both decoration and art, but although the Greeks were great observers of nature, they rarely tried to copy it directly. Typical ornamentation can be seen on the many earthenware vases that have been excavated. Patterns made of interlocking straight lines, known as frets or Greek keys, were combined in numerous ways.

Another form utilized by the Greeks was the scroll, which was used mainly as a linking device or stem for Greek floral ornament. It is difficult to identify particular flowers and plants within Greek decoration, as the motifs are stylized. Other Greek motifs include the acanthus leaf, vine leaf and grapes, palmette, ivy, and laurel.

We don't really know exactly what colors were used, as they have faded with time or have been washed away by the elements. The sculpted white marble and alabaster of the temples were once colorfully and intricately decorated. On the floors, however, many mosaics remain. Made of stone, clay, and glass, they contain rich colors, including oxide reds, azure blues, and golds.

Historic events and *legends were depicted in a decorative fashion on ancient vases.*

The Romans based their art forms on the Greek prototypes, elaborating on the scroll and creating ever more ornate and literal interpretations. A thousand years after the fall of the Roman Empire, the Renaissance in Europe marked a return to the classical vocabulary. Then, in the mid-18th century in Europe, and about 30 years later in America, the Neoclassical movement turned back to Greek and Roman models for inspiration. In Britain the architect Robert Adam created graceful adaptations of the Greek and Roman forms, and in America a similar approach prevailed in the Federal style of architecture.

As part of the eighteenth-century enthusiasm for all things classical, the proportions of rooms were determined by mathematical laws. To achieve ideal proportions, walls were divided into sections—coving, frieze, picture rail, infill or field, chair rail, dado, and baseboard—with the proportions of each section corresponding to those of the separate parts of a Greek column on a pedestal.

In modern houses, of course, these divisions have almost disappeared. For a contemporary interpretation of these sections, stenciled borders or dados are ideal and can be applied in either contrasting colors or different tones of the same color.

Though the *original colors are gone, we can still find inspiration in the architectural forms of Greece, such as these sandy, weathered columns set against a vivid blue sky.*

Right: The three *classical orders: Corinthian, Doric, and Ionic.*

This building in Charleston, *South Carolina, shows the influence of Neoclassicism in America.*

CLASSICAL COMBINATIONS

The Greek motifs feature fluid, floral patterns that can be used individually or repeated to form patterns. They are particularly suitable for creating decorative borders for walls and objects. The motifs are extremely versatile and can be used in both traditional and contemporary interiors. You can add a classic touch to any room by stenciling a formal border of Greek motifs in neutral shades at dado or picture-rail height. If you want a more modern look, try using bright, fresh colors and less formal combinations.

STENCILS

Circle

Classical leaf

Classical leaf spray

Large curl

Greek key

Square

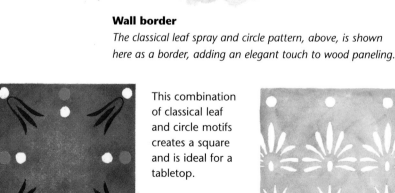

This repeat pattern can be used as a wallpaper design. Using two shades of green for the leaf spray adds extra tone to the motif.

Wall border
The classical leaf spray and circle pattern, above, is shown here as a border, adding an elegant touch to wood paneling.

This combination of classical leaf and circle motifs creates a square and is ideal for a tabletop.

A light, airy border is created by combining the circle, classical leaf spray, and the classical leaf motifs.

Greek keys do not have to be used for borders—they can stand alone as interesting motifs. Here they add a geometric element to a floral design.

Fabrics

You can coordinate fabric patterns on different furnishings by using patterns at different scales. Here the design above is used with wider spacing for curtain fabric.

Stenciling eight classical leaf motifs around a circle creates this striking decorative flower.

Cushion cover

This cushion cover uses the pattern above right to make a strong central motif.

This combination of motifs can be used within a single square or repeated to form an intricate pattern. Using three colors adds extra dynamism to the design.

GREEK-STYLE PLANT POT

Take a leaf from the Greeks and transform a simple terra-cotta pot into something special by stenciling it with these classical motifs. The classical leaf spray, also known as a palmette motif, was often used on Greek terra-cotta vases and pots, which they painted in ochers, red oxide, and black.

YOU WILL NEED

Terra-cotta plant pot

Acrylic paints: pale orange, red oxide, black

2in (50mm) flat brush

Tape measure

Pencil

Ruler

Masking tape

Stencil brush

Eraser

Flat polyurethane varnish (optional)

Varnishing brush (optional)

STENCILS

Circle

Classical leaf

Classical leaf spray

POSITIONAL GUIDE

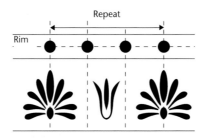

1 Using the flat brush, apply at least two coats of pale orange paint all over the outside of the pot.

2 Measure around the lower edge of the pot, and work out the spacing between the classical leaf spray motifs, leaving space to add the classical leaf motif later. Mark the repeat with vertical lines up the whole height of the pot, including the rim. Choose the height for the leaf motifs to begin, and mark this on each vertical line.

3 Position the classical leaf spray stencil so that the bottom is at your chosen height, and the vertical line goes through the center of the top leaf. Tape in place. Stencil the leaves alternately in red oxide and black, and the center in black. It may help to mask the parts of the stencil that are in the color you are not stenciling. Repeat at each vertical line.

4 Divide the repeat distance by three, and mark two vertical lines between each of the classical leaf sprays. Center the classical leaf stencil between these new vertical lines. Tape in place and stencil the outer leaves in black and the inner one in red oxide. Stencil the remaining motifs in the same way.

5 Lay a ruler across the exact center of the circle stencil, and draw a line outward to the edge of the stencil card. Match these registration lines to the vertical lines on the rim, centering the circle between the edges of the rim. Tape the stencil in place, then stencil in red oxide.

6 Move the stencil along to the next vertical line, centering it as before. Tape, then stencil in black. Continue around the rim, alternating colors.

7 Leave the paint to dry. Remove the pencil lines with an eraser. If the pot will be outside, at least two coats of varnish will be necessary.

Border **CLASSICAL LEAF TABLETOP** *patterns look as good on pieces of furniture as they do on walls. Here, two typical Greek motifs are stenciled around the edge of a round wooden table. The colors seen today on Greek monuments have faded with time, and we have tried to recreate this matte, sun-bleached look rather than the vivid colors originally used.*

1 From the center of the table draw two straight lines at right angles to each other. Draw two more lines through the center to divide it into eighths, and four more to divide it into sixteen segments.

2 Place the classical leaf stencil on one of the radiating lines, near the edge of the table. Decide how far from the edge it looks best, and mark that distance on alternate lines around the table. Position the stencil so that the bottom point is on this mark and the line goes through the middle of the central leaf. Tape in place and stencil in gray-green. Repeat around the table.

3 Decide how far in from the edge you want the circles—they look better if they are a little farther in than the classical leaf motif. Mark these points on the remaining radiating lines. Place the circle stencil on one of these marks, tape it down, and stencil in pale ocher. Reposition the stencil to do each of the other seven circles.

4 Once the paint is dry, erase the pencil guidelines. If desired, you can give the tabletop a thin, pale ocher wash, which will produce a slightly aged look. Dilute the paint 50:50 with water so it is quite thin and then lightly brush the wash over the surface with the flat brush. When the paint is dry, apply a couple of coats of varnish.

YOU WILL NEED

Round wooden table

Yardstick

Pencil

Acrylic paints: pale ocher, gray-green

Stencil brush

Masking tape

Eraser

2in (50mm) flat brush (optional)

Flat acrylic varnish

Varnishing brush

STENCILS

Circle

Classical leaf

POSITIONAL GUIDE

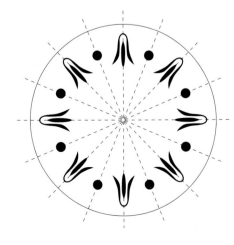

CLASSICAL WALL BORDER

Create the look of a classical Greek frieze by stenciling this elegant border at chair rail height then painting the wall above it cream and below it red oxide. The traditional practice of dividing walls into sections using chair and picture rails was originally based on the proportions of the Greek column.

YOU WILL NEED

Yardstick
Pencil
Latex paints: cream, red oxide, black
Roller or decorator's brush
Masking tape
1in (25mm) flat brush
Stencil paints: black, red
Stencil brush
Ruler
Eraser

STENCILS

Classical leaf spray

Large curl

POSITIONAL GUIDE

Repeat

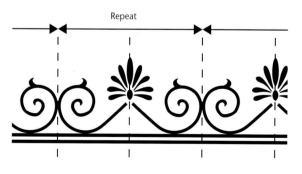

1 Using a yardstick draw a horizontal line on the wall one third of the way up from the baseboard. With a roller or decorator's brush, paint the wall above this line with cream latex. You will probably need two coats. Then apply masking tape along the line and paint the lower portion in red oxide. Peel the masking tape off while the paint is wet. Again, a second coat may be needed.

2 Mark points along the wall ¼in (6mm) above the line between the red oxide and cream. Run masking tape along the points, so the top edge of the tape is even with the marks. Mark another row of points ½in (13mm) up and run tape along so that its bottom edge lines up with these points. Use the flat brush to paint a black stripe between the two lines of tape. Remove the tape immediately.

3 When dry, repeat the process to create a ¼in- (6mm-) wide stripe ¼in (6mm) above the black line, but this time stenciling in red.

4 Run some more tape above this, with the upper edge of the tape ¾in (20mm) above the red stripe. Measure the length of your walls and work out the spacing you will need for the two border motifs. On the tape, mark the repeats all around the room and then mark points halfway between them. (Make these marks different from the others so you can tell them apart.) At each of the marked points, pencil vertical lines from the tape to the height of the border.

5 Position the large curl with the left (curved) edge against the vertical line and the bottom even with the top of the tape. Tape into position and stencil in black. Repeat for all the left-hand large curls around the entire border. When the paint on the stencil has dried, turn it over and stencil all the right-hand large curls in the same way.

6 Place a ruler across the tails of the two curls and mark where the ruler crosses the vertical line between them. Place the classical leaf spray stencil so the bottom edge is on this marked cross and the vertical line goes through the point of the central petal; tape in position. Stencil the leaves alternately in black and red, starting with black outer leaves, and with the center also in black. Repeat around the entire border. When dry, remove the pencil marks with an eraser.

MOSAIC-EFFECT FLOOR

Mosaics are synonymous with Greek decoration, from the floors and walls of ancient classical temples to the small black and white pebbles often used on the floors of Greek homes today.

YOU WILL NEED

Concrete or wooden floor

Latex paints: stone white, charcoal black

Decorator's brush

Yardstick

Pencil

Masking tape

Stencil brush

Eraser

Flat polyurethane varnish

Varnishing brush

STENCILS

Square

Greek key

1 Prepare the floor (see Basic Techniques), then apply at least two coats of the stone white latex paint. Leave to dry.

2 Starting at the center of the room, use the yardstick to draw a 3⅛in (80mm) grid over the whole floor. Don't worry if there is extra space at the edges.

3 Leave a border of two whole squares all the way around the room. By eye, center the square stencil in all the other grid squares; stencil in black latex. The fact that the stencils are not absolutely straight gives the mosaic effect.

4 Stencil a square at each corner of the floor by centering it over the cross of the grids where there are four empty squares (not within the squares). Align the Greek key stencil over the next crossing of the grid lines. Stencil and continue along each edge of the floor.

5 You can now add a border by running two parallel lines of masking tape along the outside edge of the Greek key motifs. The width of the border can vary according to how much space you have. Paint in black latex. Remove the masking tape while the paint is wet.

6 Using masking tape, make another border line between the Greek key motifs and the central panel of squares. Make this the same width as your outer border, and remove the masking tape while the paint is still wet. When dry, erase the pencil marks, clean the floor, then apply two coats of flat polyurethane varnish.

POSITIONAL GUIDE

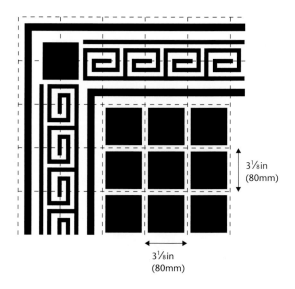

3⅛in (80mm)

3⅛in (80mm)

5

The Victorian interior is the perfect example of how motifs from different style periods can be successfully combined, to create ornate, decorative patterns. The variety of pattern in the typical Victorian home offers wonderful scope for the stenciler looking for inspiration.

VICTORIAN
inspirations

This Donegal rug *shows subtle use of color and pattern.*

The Victorian period spanned more than six decades, from 1837 to 1901. Defining it by one style is almost impossible, since its single most notable feature was the combination of a plethora of different historical revivals. This eclectic mix resulted in lavish ornamentation and a barrage of color, pattern, and texture.

Ornamentation was plundered from every source, including ancient Greece, the East, North Africa, medieval Europe, Elizabethan and Jacobean Britain, and 18th-century France. Designs were cheerfully intermixed, often with a different style in each room. For example, the feminine and frivolous style known in the United States as "Second Rococo" was favored in boudoirs and drawing rooms. The grand, stately, and opulent "Beaux-Arts" style was fashionable in very wealthy homes.

Acanthus scrolls, keys and classical leaf sprays, Gothic arches, thistles and fleurs-de-lis, and images of flowers,

This wallpaper design *uses stylized floral motifs in an almost Islamic fashion.*

plants, birds, and animals were all popular in the Victorian era. These motifs and patterns would be incorporated in every aspect of the home—no surface was left bare.

Patterned, textured wallpapers were popular, often with two or three on one wall, framed by architectural elements such as molded coving, picture rails, and chair rails. Sometimes the frieze (above the picture rail) and ceiling were whitewashed, but at other times the frieze and the infill (between the picture rail and chair rail) would be in two different designs, such as birds and fruit, or trellises and flowers. The area below the chair rail might be painted or covered with embossed wallpaper. Some manufacturers offered sets of coordinating wallpapers.

Stenciling was often used. Ceilings were sometimes stenciled, as were borders and friezes. Baseboards and other woodwork might be stenciled to match fabrics or wallpapers used in the room. Speciality paint finishes were also commonly used on walls, woodwork, and coves.

Rich, ornate, draped fabric covered virtually everything, including doors, chimney pieces, even pianos. Rooms were filled with highly-decorated furniture, overstuffed upholstery with lavish trimmings, dark wood, plants, and treasures collected from far and wide. With gilt-framed family portraits on the walls and gently glowing gas light, oil lamps, or candles, the atmosphere was either very cozy or somewhat claustrophobic, depending on your taste.

The Victorians were great lovers of color, using many hues including bottle green, gold, burgundy, mahogany, bright

Striking red

was used by William de Morgan for this fantastical beast, inspired by medieval art.

yellow, violet, magenta, turquoise, and lapis lazuli. Crimson and Etruscan or Pompeian red were both fashionable for dining rooms, and were combined with dark woodwork and floorboards, gilt frames and objects, and sumptuous fabrics.

The Victorian period provides a good example of how interpreting motifs differently, using alternative color schemes, and combining various patterns and textures, can create a look that feels very different from the original. The soft earth pigments of the Greek palette were rejected in favor of bold, vibrant colors using the newly-invented synthetic dyes.

For the projects in this chapter we have used motifs from the Greek theme—the classical leaf spray, Greek key, large curl, and circle—but altered the scale and formations to create panels of repeat elements, and stenciled them in typically Victorian colors. Linking motifs such as the Greek key or the scroll (created from a pair of large curl motifs) could be combined to create borders for use at chair-rail or picture-rail height.

It is easy to find objects to stencil, as the Victorians were such collectors of diverse objects that almost anything goes. Try mixing embroidered and stenciled fabrics using flower, bird, or animal motifs for pillow covers or wall hangings. Or stencil linking scrolls with classical leaf sprays in gold on heavy, dark mirror frames.

A watercolor painting

of a Viennese interior of about 1850, showing that Victorian style was popular all across Europe.

VICTORIAN COMBINATIONS

Victorian decorative work was generally contained within a frame, such as paneling, a dado, or a tile. Popular in this period were border designs, wallpapers based on grids, and individual emblems in a variety of colors. The Victorian motifs here can be combined to make striking emblems and patterns that are particularly effective for decorating a wide variety of objects in a contemporary interior, such as trays, chair backs, wallpaper, door panels, and flooring.

STENCILS

Greek key

Simple curl

Circle

Medieval leaf spray

Kite

Classical leaf spray

Classical leaf

Chair back
Both wooden and fabric panels in dining chairs can be decorated, here with the panel design at right. Remember to fix fabric paints as necessary.

This elegant emblem is created from sprigs, circles, kites, and fleurs-de-lis. Used alone it is a panel pattern, but if used over a grid it would link to form a lattice pattern.

This gentle design featuring circle, sprig, kite, and fleur-de-lis motifs resembles a star or a snow flake. It is ideal for wall or floor tiles.

This pattern is effective as a frame as well as a border.

Place mat
To coordinate the decor of a whole room, link accessories of all sizes, such as place mats, by decorating them with the border pattern at top left.

This light, airy design is effective as a border or as a widely spaced repeat.

Floorboards
Border patterns, such as the one above right, can be used on plain floorboards— this takes advantage of their linear form.

The kites, circles, and sprigs are linked with simple curls, giving a light, fresh look that would be particularly suited to curtain fabric.

This elegant emblem is formed from a combination of sprig, circle, and kite motifs radiating from a central image.

PANELED WALL DESIGN

The Victorians loved mixing style periods, and the eclectic mixture of motifs in this elaborate wall design certainly adds its appeal. Either copy it exactly, perhaps combining it with the Victorian-style border on page 67, or simplify it if you prefer. The rich colors are typically Victorian but could be lightened.

YOU WILL NEED

Steel tape measure

Pencil

Masking tape

Latex paints: dark forest green, medium green, pale green (optional)

Decorator's brush or roller

Large sheet of Mylar or oiled manila stencil card

Fiber-tip pen

Ruler

Cutting mat

craft knife or mat knife

Stencil paints: yellow ocher, red oxide

Stencil brush

POSITIONAL GUIDE

Center

2in (50mm)

1in (25mm)

STENCILS

Greek key

Kite

Classical leaf

Circle

Large curl

Medieval leaf spray

Classical leaf spray

Paint your wall with medium green latex; leave to dry. Mark points one-third of the way up and run masking tape around with the lower edge of the tape along the points. Paint below the tape with dark forest green and remove the tape. Leave to dry.

1 To make a master stencil (see Basic Techniques) you need stencil card or mylar that is tall enough to fill the dark green area; if it isn't, divide the design in half and use two pieces. Work out the overall width of the design and divide this measurement into the distance around the room, adjusting the spacing between motifs so that it will fit exactly (see Basic Techniques).

2 Divide the height of the dark green area by the length of the Greek key motif to see how many Greek keys will fit. If they do not fit exactly, leave a gap at the top and bottom. Using a fiber-tip pen to draw through the stencil onto the master stencil card, mark a column of Greek keys near one edge. Keep the independent line of the motif on the outside.

3 Leaving enough room on the stencil card for two large curl motifs side by side, with a space on either side, draw another column of Greek keys, with the independent line on the outside. Now mark the vertical center line between the two Greek key columns.

4 Following the grid, place the large curl stencil level with the bottom of the Greek keys, with the end of the curl horizontal. The tip of the curl should be 2in (50mm) away from the center line. Draw through the stencil; turn it over and draw a mirror image on the other side of the center line. With a ruler, join the ends of these two stencils together in a straight line.

5 Draw another pair of large curls above the first pair. This time tilt them so that the end line is at 45 degrees to the horizontal. Position them so that there is a 1in (25mm) gap between the ends. Draw a third pair above these, but with the curls facing downward and the tips meeting.

6 Place the classical leaf spray stencil above the top curls with the middle of the leaf spray on the vertical central line, as on the grid; draw through it.

7 Centering your stencils on the central line, draw the classical leaf in the space between the curls at the bottom, pointing upward. Do a similar one between the top curls, but pointing downward. Still on the central vertical add kite shapes above and below the central pair of curls, pointing upward and downward respectively.

8 Draw through the circle stencil, placing it on each side of the vertical center line, halfway out toward the Greek keys, and halfway between the bottom curl and the one above it. Also draw a circle on the center line, just above the bottom pair of curls.

9 Draw only the inner leaf of the medieval leaf spray between the two large curls in the middle. Draw the outer leaves higher up in the spaces between the large curls and the upper kite motif. Repeat the outer leaves at the outer edges of the gaps between tiers, as shown on the grid.

10 Once the design is drawn on the master stencil, cut out each shape (see Basic Techniques). Mark the positions of the full design repeat around the room, then tape the master stencil in place. You can use the two colors for different components of the whole stencil design, but make sure that you keep them symmetrical. Stencil the entire design before moving on.

WOODEN NAPKIN RINGS

Very simple shapes—a kite and a circle—have been used to create these distinctive napkin rings. You could decorate a whole set of rings with different combinations or arrangements of these motifs. Instead of stenciling bright colors onto painted wood, as here, you could use brown paint on natural wood for a marquetry effect.

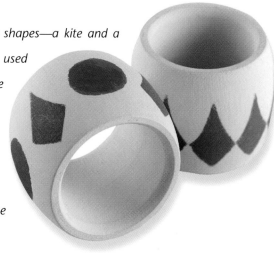

YOU WILL NEED

Wooden napkin rings

Stencil paints: cream, forest green, vermilion red

2in (50mm) flat brush

Tape measure

Pencil

Masking tape

Stencil brush

Eraser

Satin acrylic varnish

Varnishing brush

STENCILS

Kite

Circle

1 Using the flat brush, apply two or three coats of cream paint all over the napkin rings.

2 When the paint is dry, measure around the rings with the tape measure. Divide by the width of the kite motif, to find the number of motifs that will fit in. If it does not fit exactly, divide the remainder by the number of motifs, for the exact space between motifs. Pencil the repeats onto the ring.

3 Measure the height of the ring and divide by three. Pencil a line around the ring one-third of the distance from the edge. Tape the kite stencil at each repeat mark, with its two sidepoints resting on the pencil line, and stencil in green.

4 For the kite-and-circle napkin ring, divide the distance around the ring by the combined width of the circle and kite together; this gives you the number of repeats. Divide any remainder by the number of repeats to give some space between the motifs. Measure out and mark the position of the repeats around the ring.

5 Mark a line around the ring at one third of the height as for the previous design. Tape the kite stencil in place; stencil in green. Mark another line at half the width and center the circle over this line, halfway between each kite. Stencil in vermilion red.

6 When dry, erase the pencil marks and apply a coat of varnish to all the rings.

An alternative colorway for these napkin rings is shown on page 69.

POSITIONAL GUIDES

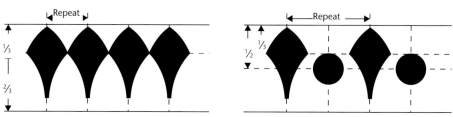

VICTORIAN STYLE BORDER

The Victorians used chair rails and picture rails to improve the proportions of their walls and rooms. If your home has chair rails you could run this border alongside them, but if it does not, this border will create a similar effect. Try combining it with the wall design on pages 64–65.

1 Mark points one-third of the way up the wall, all around the room. Run masking tape around the room with the upper edge even with the marked points. Mark additional points 3½in (90mm) above the upper edge of the tape. Run more tape around the room, with the lower edge even with the new marks.

2 Using the flat brush and dark forest green latex, paint the area between the two lines of tape, to create a background for the stenciled motifs. Remove the masking tape before the paint dries.

3 Measure the distance around the room, and divide it by the repeat—the total width of the medieval leaf spray, kite, space between them and space before the next stencil. If it doesn't fit exactly, adjust the spacing (see Basic Techniques). Mark the positions of the motifs along the border at the top and the bottom of the band. Finally, mark the halfway line between the top and bottom of the band at each point where the kites will be stenciled.

4 Position the medieval leaf spray stencil so that its top point and the center of the base are even with the marks on the wall, and the motif is centered vertically on the band. Stencil in yellow ocher and red oxide, as shown in the photograph. Repeat all around the border.

5 Now line up the kite motif so that its widest point sits on the halfway line and it is centered between the other motifs. Stencil in yellow ocher. Repeat all around the border. When the paint is dry erase the pencil lines.

YOU WILL NEED

Steel tape measure

Pencil

Masking tape

Latex paint: dark forest green

2in (50mm) flat brush

Stencil paints: yellow ocher, red oxide

Stencil brush

Eraser

STENCILS

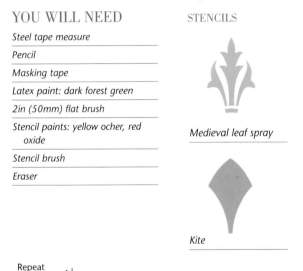

Medieval leaf spray

Kite

POSITIONAL GUIDE

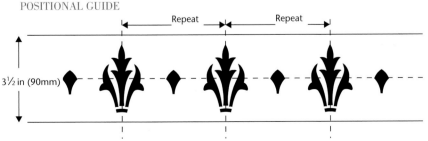

Repeat   Repeat

3½ in (90mm)

BLACK AND GOLD MIRROR FRAME

This imposing mirror frame with its elegant black and gold border was once a run-of-the-mill wooden frame. Stenciling with just two leaf spray motifs, punctuated with circles, has created this ornate border, and the effect of the gold paint (over burnt umber) against a black background more than lives up to it.

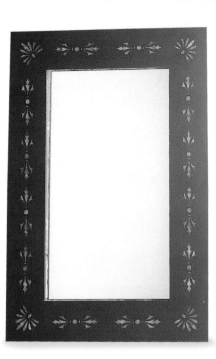

YOU WILL NEED

Wooden mirror frame

Latex paint: charcoal black

Stencil paint: burnt umber, gold

2in (50mm) flat brush

Masking tape

Ruler

Stencil brush

Pencil

Eraser

Satin acrylic varnish

Varnishing brush

STENCILS

Classical leaf spray

Medieval leaf spray

Circle

POSITIONAL GUIDE

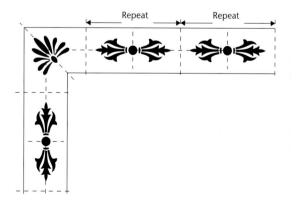

1 Prepare the surface (see Basic Techniques) then paint two coats of charcoal black latex, with the flat brush.

2 When dry, place a ruler diagonally across one corner, and lay the classical leaf spray stencil over it so that the ruler goes through the center. Tape the stencil down and remove the ruler. Stencil in burnt umber. Repeat this process in each corner.

3 Lightly pencil a line dividing each side of the frame in half along its length. Work out the number of repeats and their spacing for the size of your frame (see Basic Techniques), and mark these along the center lines.

4 Draw a line across the center of the circle stencil to give you a registration line. Line it up on the pencil line along the center of the frame halfway between your repeat marks. Tape and stencil in burnt umber. Repeat all around the frame.

5 On one side of this circle, position the medieval leaf spray stencil so that the center line cuts through the middle of it. Stencil in burnt umber. When dry, turn the stencil over and stencil a mirror image on the other side of the circle in burnt umber. Repeat all around the frame.

6 Now put the appropriate stencil back over each burnt umber motif, lining it up by eye, and stencil lightly with gold. When the paint is dry, erase the guidelines and

6

Indian interiors combine rich colors and textures with elaborate decoration—finely embroidered curtains, stenciled walls, carved and inlaid furniture, intricate silver ornaments, beautiful rugs and wall hangings—providing lots of inspiration for the creative stenciler.

INDIAN
inspirations

The contrasting colors *used in this fabric print are typical of Indian textiles.*

India is one of the largest countries in the world, and was home to some of the world's most ancient civilizations. It was the crossroads of Asia, through which many migrations passed, some of them settling there, and for many centuries it was ruled by foreigners. With such a rich and varied history and a population made up of many different cultures, it is not surprising that Indian art is very diverse. The influence of foreign rule can be seen in the art forms—it was heavily influenced by Arabian art, which is rigid and ordered, and by Persian art, which is much more fluid—but Indian artists and craftsmen also have their own traditions.

The most striking feature of India is the brilliant array of colors that adorn everyone and everything. From the people and buildings to the buses and taxis, and even the elephants and camels, no surface is left undecorated. Color and ornament are intrinsic to everyday life in India.

We have taken our inspiration from India's distinctive ornament and rich color. Using the stencils for a traditional sprig, a simple curled stem, and a symmetrical leaf spray, you can create a variety of patterns and borders. Other motifs commonly used in India include the

The Palace of the Four
Winds in Jaipur, which was built in 1799.

sacred lotus flower and the feathery palmette now know, as paisley. Designs are often set out with a large central motif—perhaps a flowering tree—surrounded by scattered sprigs. This is then framed with any number of borders made up of linking, curling leaves and flowers.

In India, the production of any object is looked on as the creation of an art form; the maker is an artist, not simply a worker on an assembly line. Even basic objects have surface decoration to enhance the shape and form in a simple yet stylish manner. The decoration reflects the size and shape of the object, with small, linking motifs applied to narrow areas and larger, more formal patterns used on the main body.

India has one of the widest ranges of handicrafts in the world (stenciling, for example, has been done since around AD 600, the technique having spread from China with the opening of trade routes). Skilled work is produced in all media, but India's greatest export is textiles. Block printing, embroidery, tie-dyeing, or quilting is found on everything from saris to wall hangings. The weaves and designs vary from region to region, depending on the culture, religion, and social needs of each area. However, the distinguishing feature common to all Indian textiles is the abundance and richness of color; vibrant red, saffron, orange, emerald,

The paisley motifs *on this scarf are part of the classical repertoire of Indian decoration.*

henna green, peacock blue, maroon, and ocher are all created with simple vegetable dyes.

You could use vegetable dyes on plain white cotton or muslin curtains, bed linen, and pillow and cushion covers prior to stenciling them.

Washing machine dyes are a simple alternative to natural dyes, or you could leave the fabric white and then stencil with gold or amber, emulating the fine gold chainstitching found on some Indian textiles. For traditional Indian-style curtains, stencil floral motifs arranged in a geometric pattern across the fabric and a border along the lower edge.

Indian-style borders could also be stenciled on whitewashed walls around doors and windows, around picture frames, along chair backs, or around tabletops (perhaps combined with a central floral motif). Add some low wooden chairs and stools carved or inlaid with metal, bone, or other woods—or stenciled to create a similar effect—and scatter embroidered or stenciled floor pillows around the room.

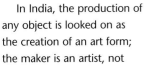

Modern craft- *makers are inspired by the colors of India, as in this mosaic-covered hand mirror.*

The flattened perspective *in this 19th-century painting gives it a decorative effect.*

INDIAN COMBINATIONS

The Indian motifs are extremely flexible and can be used to create rigid, formal patterns as well as beautiful, fluid designs. The curl is an excellent linking device for the leaf-spray motif, and the sprig motif adds a light touch to repeat patterns. You can achieve a wide variety of effects by choosing color schemes carefully. Although bright contrasting colors are ideal for Indian motifs, you can create a more subtle effect by using subdued complementary colors.

STENCILS

Indian leaf spray

Simple curl

Sprig

Circle

Kite

This intricate combination of the Indian leaf spray and sprig motifs can be used as a border or on fabric.

Wall pattern
Adapting the design above for a wall pattern, the addition of a textured, mottled background adds interest.

The Indian leaf spray and sprig motifs are combined to create a rich and elegant repeat pattern.

Using a grid of squares divided by diagonal lines, a repeat pattern is created which is both light and dynamic.

Magazine rack

Don't be afraid to use the larger motifs, even on quite small objects. The Indian leaf spray and simple curl pattern, right, has been used on a magazine rack to brighten it up.

This beautiful creeping-vine design featuring the simple curl and the Indian leaf spray motifs is made all the more striking by the use of bold, contrasting colors.

Chair cover

The panel pattern to the left could be used as a single motif on a chair seat, and also extends into a linear pattern for tall chair backs.

The strong symmetry in this panel design is a common feature of pattern creation in every culture.

This swirling emblem was created from one simple motif: the sprig. It can be used on its own or dotted sparsely across fabric or a wall.

LEAF AND SPRIG CURTAINS

Look to the East and create rich, sumptuous fabrics. This design is based on the sprig and Indian leaf spray, with a border derived from a mirror image of the motifs. We stenciled the pattern only on the bottom third of the curtain as sari fabric is often decorated just along the lower portion.

YOU WILL NEED

Readymade white muslin curtains

Washing machine dye: burgundy

Iron

Sheet of plastic to protect work surface

Masking tape

Tape measure

Fabric paint: gold

Stencil brush

Two rulers

STENCILS

Indian leaf spray   Sprig

POSITIONAL GUIDE

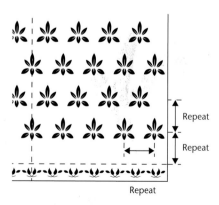

Repeat

Repeat

Repeat

1 Dye the curtains, following the manufacturer's directions, then iron them. Lay one curtain flat over a sheet of plastic, to protect your surface. Tape the fabric in place to keep it taut.

2 For the border, stencil the first sprig horizontally at the center of the curtain's hem with gold fabric paint. Turn the stencil over and position it by eye, with the stem crossing over the first one and a gap between the leaves; stencil.

3 For the next motif, turn the stencil back over to the original direction and place it close to the last one. You may find it easier to cut a second, identical stencil, otherwise each time you need to flip the stencil over you will have to wait for the paint to dry. Stencil the entire border in this way, using the bottom edge of the curtain as a guide to keep it straight.

4 For the main pattern, decide on the spacing (it should be quite wide) and measure up from the border by this amount. Place

the point of the central petal of the Indian leaf spray stencil at this height; stencil the first flower.

5 With one ruler, measure the same distance across the width from the center of that flower, and with a second ruler measure this distance up from the border. Place the point of the central petal on the spot where the two rulers meet; stencil. Continue in this way until the first row is complete.

6 Place one ruler horizontally across the last two flowers, and use the other ruler to measure the standard distance upward from the halfway point between them. Position the stencil on this spot as before, stencil the motif, then continue across the row. The remaining rows are easier, as you can position the ruler from alternate rows and measure a double space upward.

7 If the manufacturer's instructions require it, fix the fabric paint with an iron.

POSITIONAL GUIDE

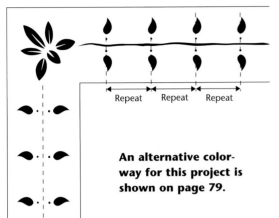

Repeat   Repeat   Repeat

An alternative color-way for this project is shown on page 79.

Stenciling is an excellent way to give worn-out old picture frames a new lease on life. We deliberately aimed for a rough, handmade look, with a folk-art feel to the motifs. Adding some simple freehand painted lines gives it further interest.

GREEN LEAF PICTURE FRAME

YOU WILL NEED

Wooden picture frame

Piece of hardboard cut to size (optional)

Wood glue (optional)

Latex paint: white

2in (50mm) flat brush

Pencil

Masking tape

Stencil paint: jade green

Stencil brush

Fine artist's brush

Eraser

Flat acrylic varnish

Varnishing brush

STENCILS

Indian leaf spray

Sprig

1 Prepare the surface (see Basic Techniques). If the frame is not wide enough to decorate, you can extend it by gluing hardboard over the front so that the hardboard extends beyond the frame. Your local lumberyard should be able to cut the shape for you. This border needs a width of at least 5in (125mm). Apply two or three coats of white paint with the flat brush.

2 When dry, pencil a line along the center of each side. Place the Indian leaf spray stencil in one corner, with the bottom leaves on the pencil lines. Stencil in jade green. Repeat at each corner.

3 Using a fine brush, paint a jade green line running down the center of each side of the frame, stopping just short of the Indian leaf spray. To keep the line straight, rest one finger on the outside of the frame as you drag your hand down. Adding a little nodule every few inches will give it an organic, twig-like appearance.

4 With masking tape, mask out the small leaf and the stem on the sprig stencil. Calculate your repeat distance—you will want it to be at least 2in (50mm). Place the stencil at the bottom of one side of the frame, about ⅜in (10mm) to the left of the painted line. Stencil a green leaf, then continue around the whole frame.

5 When dry, turn the stencil over and do the same thing up the right side of the line.

6 Using the fine brush, paint a dot in the space between each leaf and the jade line, in line with the inner tip of each leaf. When dry, erase the pencil marks and apply a single coat of varnish.

INLAY-STYLE CHEST

Inspired by the intricate inlaid metal designs that adorn some Indian furniture, this very basic wooden chest has been transformed through the use of gold paint into a piece that looks complex and detailed. In fact, most Indian furniture is simple like this, and the ornamentation comes from applied decoration or carving.

YOU WILL NEED

Wooden chest

Ruler

Pencil

Tape measure

Masking tape

1in (25mm) flat brush

Stencil paint: gold

Stencil brush

Eraser

Acrylic varnish

Varnishing brush

STENCILS

Simple curl

Indian leaf spray

Sprig

POSITIONAL GUIDES

Top

Front   Center line

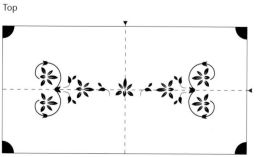

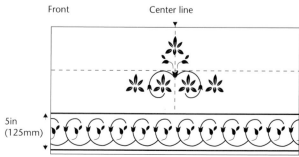

5in
(125mm)

1 Prepare the wood surface (see Basic Techniques). Measure out and draw lines for the border ¼in (6mm) apart around the sides of the chest near the bottom, and two more lines the same distance apart 5in (125mm) above this. Run masking tape outside the lines. With the flat brush, apply gold paint between the pairs of tape lines; remove the tape immediately.

2 On the top, measure out and draw a line ¼in (6mm) from each edge. Run tape outside the lines. Carefully paint the strip gold then remove the tape. At each corner, draw around one-quarter of a circular object to produce a curve, and fill in with gold paint.

3 Measure the width of the sides, and work out the spacing between the repeats of the simple curl motif border. Centering the stencil between the two stripes, stencil simple curls all around the sides.

4 Place the sprig stencil so the top leaf is ⅜in (10mm) below the point that curls inward on the simple curl motif and so the curved stem of the sprig points toward the other point of the curl. Stencil a sprig inside each curl all the way around the border.

5 On both the short sides of the chest, measure halfway between the two ends, and halfway between the upper stripe and the top. Mark this center point with a small cross formed by a vertical and a horizontal line. Stencil one leaf spray on the smaller sides of the chest, with the base of its top leaf touching the pencil cross. Stencil two more leaf sprays either side, so that there is a 2in (50mm) gap between the leaves.

6 On the front panel, draw a pencil line horizontally across, halfway between the top of the border and the top of the panel. Mark the center point of this line. Stencil a curl and a mirror-image curl (produced by turning the stencil over) with the points touching, below the center point. The top of the curl should just be touching the horizontal halfway-line.

7 Above these curls, stencil a sprig and a mirror-image sprig, with the bottom of each on the halfway line and about ½in (13mm) from the center point. About 1in (25mm) above them stencil another leaf spray. Add a leaf spray within each of the curls, making sure they line up with each other. About ⅜in (10mm) to each side of the two curls, stencil two more leaf sprays; use a ruler to line up the bottoms with the leaf sprays within the curls.

8 For the top of the chest, mark the center point with a cross, then also mark points halfway between that point and each side. Stencil a leaf spray at the center mark. At one of the other two marks, stencil a curl and a mirror image curl, both with leaf sprays inside, a sprig and mirror-image sprig, and then a leaf spray—in other words, as for the front panel but without the two outer leaf sprays. The complete design should appear to "point" to the center. At the other mark do the same thing, but in reverse, so it too "points" to the center. Finally, between these and the center leaf spray, stencil a sprig and a mirror-image sprig.

9 To make the various groups of motifs link more neatly, the final stage is to use the little leaf motif which appears on the curl stencil. Use the complete stencil, but just apply paint across the leaf section of the stencil. Paint this little motif over the joins of the curl motifs on the front and top of the chest, and also twice on the short sides as a separate motif halfway between the leaf curls. When all the gold paint is dry, erase the pencil marks and varnish the chest.

Side   Center line

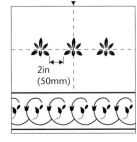

2in
(50mm)

SAFFRON PILLOW COVER

Using rich saffron, crimson, jade, turquoise, and gold in the home will create a sumptuous atmosphere.

Color is the most striking feature of Indian design, but if you don't want a multitude of colors and patterns, bring in small splashes of color on curtains and pillow covers.

YOU WILL NEED

White pillow cover

Washing machine dye: saffron or mustard

Iron

Sheet of plastic to protect work surface

Masking tape

Tape measure

Fabric paint: crimson

Stencil brush

Two rulers

STENCILS

Simple curl

Sprig

Indian leaf spray

1 Dye the pillow cover, following the manufacturer's directions, and iron it. Protect your work surface with plastic, and tape the fabric down tautly.

2 The border is based on the simple curl motif. Measure the cover and work out the spacing to fit the curls in neatly. Using the crimson fabric paint, stencil the first curl at one corner, leaving enough space for the sprig to be stenciled later. When dry, flip and turn the stencil upside down and stencil the next repeat. Turn it back and stencil again, and continue in this way along the border.

3 Stencil the Indian leaf spray inside each curl, lining up the small bottom leaf with the tip of the curl that points inward. When dry, flip and turn the leaf spray stencil upside down for the next one, and continue in this way.

4 Position the sprig stencil with the stem about 3/8in (10mm) from the inward-pointing curve of the simple curl; stencil. Turn it upside down for the next one, and repeat.

5 The motif of the main pattern is made up of the sprig and a mirror-image of it, with the stems crossing. The motifs are arranged in a checkerboard pattern (see grid). Decide on the spacing between motifs, and the spacing between rows. Use two rulers as in the Leaf and Sprig Curtains project (see page 74) to position each motif before stenciling it.

6 Fix the paints with an iron, following the manufacurer's directions.

POSITIONAL GUIDE

7

Japanese ornament is never symmetrical and follows very fluid forms. Composition and balance in both color and form, rather than careful measuring, are the key elements. Even the most pictorial work has a decorative quality deriving from the grace of the lines.

JAPANESE
inspirations

A few lines create the *form of a fish, and the calligraphy also serves a decorative purpose in this beautiful scroll painting.*

Japanese art is the art of the calligrapher—the artist learns to draw as he learns to write: by repeating lines and marks. The image is produced with just a few carefully placed strokes re-creating the most delicate of images. The work is not representational but a mere suggestion of nature. The flat depiction of images combined with the grace of the lines lends a unique decorative quality even to highly pictorial work.

This high degree of skill and close attention to detail are brought to bear on all pieces of work, however utilitarian. As a result, it is hard to separate the design from the process, as the artist and workman are one and the same.

The fundamental inspiration is nature. Motifs generally fall into the following categories: flowers (such as the chrysanthemum, peony, or water lily); birds (like the crane, hawk, or kingfisher); fish and shellfish (for example, the carp, lobster, or crab); and insects (such as the grasshopper, cricket, or wasp). However, the most common image associated with Japanese art has to be bamboo, which symbolizes longevity and fullness of life. Bamboo stalk and leaf stencils are used in the projects in this chapter.

Another distinctive characteristic of Japanese ornamentation is the quiet and refined color range, which includes soft, natural tones of gold, sandy yellow, brown, cream, and shades of green from sage to olive. Harmonies rather than contrasts are used.

Japanese design tends to avoid any appearance of symmetry. When Japanese artists are forming a pattern, the design is started not in the center but slightly off-center; the composition is then balanced by another motif or color. Likewise, a design is not divided into equal parts as a Western design is.

Stenciling spread to Japan from China. Fabric stencil dyeing (applying a resist through a stencil, then hand dyeing the uncovered areas) is still a popular art form in Japan today, typically using indigo.

This seeming simplicity in Japanese design lends itself perfectly to contemporary applications. For example, in two of the projects in this chapter you can stencil subtle

An intricately-decorated *set of boxes uses deep red, black, and gold laquerwork.*

bamboo leaves floating across a wall or a paper screen. Another creates a lacquer-effect box in black and gold. These techniques could be adapted to create an imitation lacquerwork dining table and chairs, a paper window shade, or many other simple but elegant items. Japanese decoration lends itself to creative interpretation, so experiment with painterly compositions for your home.

Even practical
objects were decorated, as with the herons gliding across this fan.

A free-flowing
floral design is used here on a kimono.

JAPANESE COMBINATIONS

A key feature of Japanese design is the use of fluid and geometric forms without the symmetry commonly found in the decorative work of other cultures. A number of dynamic wall designs can be created using the linear bamboo stalk and the contrasting bamboo leaf. You can make a design more abstract by simply eliminating a section of the motif. Alternatively you can make compositions less random by framing them with the formal key or the linear stalk motifs. Different looks can be achieved by using a variety of colors ranging from subtle ivory and gold to bold white and red.

STENCILS

Greek key

Bamboo stalks

Bamboo leaf

Marguerite

Natural leaf

Turning and rotating a single motif will allow you to create patterns that are interesting without being too fussy.

Bed cover
The pattern on the left, used here on a bed cover, has a fresh and natural look due to the use of green and brown fabric paints.

Stenciled in a square, this combination of floral motifs looks efffective when used as a border for a cushion cover or tabletop.

Created with the marguerite and bamboo leaf motifs, this diagonal repeat makes a very effective wallpaper pattern.

Window shade

The full diagonal impact of the pattern at top right is seen on this window shade

This attractive diagonal repeat featuring the bamboo leaf and stalk motifs is effective both over a wide area such as wallpaper or within a smaller area as shown here.

Repeating and flipping the bamboo leaf motif makes a striking pattern that is ideal for fabric.

Bathrobe

Although the colors are not true to nature, the effect of using a pale bamboo motif brightens a rather dark-colored bathrobe.

A strong color contrast adds extra interest to this use of the bamboo stalk and marguerite motifs.

ORIENTAL SCREEN

Screens are very appropriate for a Japanese style of decor. Translucent handmade paper in the panels give it many different appearances as light conditions change. The painterly approach of the bamboo contrasts beautifully with the Greek key surround, which frames the whole design.

YOU WILL NEED

Screen with panels (see step 1)

Primer

2in (50mm) flat brush

Latex paint: dark olive green

Tape measure

Pencil

Spray paints: brown, beige

Masking tape

Satin acrylic varnish

Varnishing brush

Plain paper

Translucent handmade paper
    (see step 3)

Sheet of plastic to protect work
    surface

Newspaper

Staple gun

Thin strips of braid (optional)

Fabric glue (optional)

STENCILS

Greek key

Bamboo stalks

Bamboo leaf

SUGGESTED FREEHAND PATTERN

Center line

1 If you don't have a suitable screen, you could ask a lumberyard to cut wooden panels to size and to cut out the centers. (Make sure that the frame is wide enough for the Greek key motif.) Then all you have to do is attach pairs of hinges at the top and bottom of adjacent panels.

2 Using the flat brush, prime the wood and apply two coats of dark olive green latex paint. Mark the center point between the top and bottom of the frame. Center the Greek key stencil on this point, and stencil in brown spray paint (see Basic Techniques). Continue stenciling along the frame, then do the same on the opposite side. Repeat for the other panels. In each case, try to stop in line with the other stopping points. When dry, apply one coat of varnish and leave the varnish to dry.

3 Experiment with the arrangement of the bamboo stalks and leaves on sheets of plain paper, sketching various possibilities. The handmade paper for each panel will need to be at least 1½in (40mm) longer and the same amount wider than the cutout in each frame.

4 Once you have decided on the design, lay the hand made paper on a flat surface (protected with a sheet of plastic) in a well-ventilated room, and begin stenciling. Tape newspaper around the stencil, as the spray tends to cover quite a wide area. Stencil the bamboo stalks in brown or beige, grouping the stalks and turning the stencil over or upside down as you spray the repeats, to avoid creating a repetitive pattern. Leave some open spaces, rather than covering the whole area.

5 Once there is a scattering of stalks, begin stenciling the leaves in those areas, again in beige and brown. Here, too, turn the stencil over or upside down.

6 The other two panels don't have to be identical, but if you want them to be, simply lay the next panel over the stenciled one, and lightly pencil the leaves and stalks positions as a guide.

7 When the paint is dry, lay the screen flat on the floor, face down, and center the stenciled paper over the cutouts. Stretch the paper so it is taut and straight, and staple it to the back of the screen. If desired, glue thin strips of braid over the staples to cover them up.

LACQUER-EFFECT BOX

Black Japanese lacquer-work, with its gilt highlights, was the inspiration for this lovely box. Although the marguerite and natural leaf motifs are positioned seemingly at random, there is more artistry and planning behind their arrangement than is apparent.

SUGGESTED FREEHAND PATTERN

YOU WILL NEED

Wooden box

Acrylic paints: black, gold

2in (50mm) flat brush

Pencil

Paper

Masking tape

Stencil brush

High gloss polyurethane varnish

Varnishing brush

STENCILS

Marguerite

Natural leaf

1 Using the flat brush, apply black paint over the whole box. Leave to dry. You will probably need to apply two or more coats in order to achieve the full depth of color.

2 While the paint is drying, you can begin planning the design. There is no formal structure to follow, so try out some arrangements of the two motifs on paper until you find a composition you are happy with. Think of the box as a whole, rather than each surface as an unrelated plane. Do not attempt to cover the whole surface or to regiment the motifs into a rigid pattern. Think of it more in terms of clusters and empty spaces—these positive and negative spaces will have a "tension" between them that makes the design more stimulating.

3 Once you are happy with the design, use your drawings as a guide to begin stenciling in gold with the two stencils. Leave the paint thinner in some areas than others, to produce a slightly aged look.

4 Stencil your way around the box, continuing the motifs around the corners in order to link each side of the box.

5 Apply two or three coats of varnish to imitate the high gloss of Japanese lacquerwork. Be sure to allow it to dry completely before applying the next coat.

BAMBOO TABLE-TOP

Create a pretty top for any coffee table using traditional Japanese bamboo motifs. Our table had bamboo legs but a modern square table would be suitable, too, as you could stencil bamboo stems up the legs. We have used neutral colors, but black and gold would be a striking alternative.

1 Prepare the surface (see Basic Techniques). Using the flat brush, apply two or three coats of dark brown latex paint to the tabletop.

2 When the paint is dry, place the bamboo stalk stencil near (but not actually in) one corner, lining it up with the edge of the table. Stencil in sandy yellow, but only through the larger stalk (if necessary, mask off the other stalk temporarily with tape).

3 When dry, turn the stencil over so that the narrower ends of the stalks are facing the opposite way. Place the stencil so that the smaller stalk is centered above the larger stalk you have already stenciled. Stencil the smaller stalk in sandy yellow.

4 Turn the stencil back to the original direction, move it along, and stencil through the larger stalk once more. Continue in this way around the table, creating an outer border of small stalks running clockwise around the table and an inner border of large stalks running counterclockwise.

5 Once the border has dried, place the bamboo leaf stencil in one corner so that the points of the leaves point inward. Stencil in sandy yellow, then repeat for the other corners, flipping the stencil over to give extra variety.

6 When dry, apply two coats of high-gloss polyurethane varnish to give the table the look of Japanese lacquerwork.

YOU WILL NEED

Coffee table

Latex paint: dark brown

2in (50mm) flat brush

Masking tape

Stencil paint: sandy yellow

Stencil brush

High-gloss polyurethane varnish

Varnishing brush

STENCILS

Bamboo stalk

Bamboo leaf

POSITIONAL GUIDE

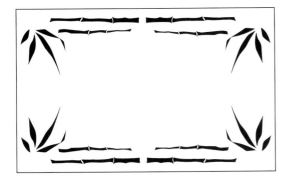

BAMBOO WALL DESIGN

The neutral colors and clean lines of Japanese designs lend themselves well to a contemporary interpretation. This wall design, in subtle shades of brown against a cream background, has a quiet, calm look as if the bamboo is gently swaying in the breeze.

YOU WILL NEED

Latex paint: cream

Decorator's brush or roller

Paper (optional)

Pencil (optional)

Newspaper

Masking tape

Spray paints: brown, beige

STENCILS

Bamboo leaf

Bamboo stalk

1 Paint the walls with cream-colored latex paint, using the decorator's brush or roller. The design is stenciled onto the wall as a freehand pattern. Sketch your composition on paper beforehand to use as a guide when stenciling.

2 Protect your surfaces by taping newspaper over them, because spray paints cover quite a wide area. Open the windows so that the room is well ventilated.

3 Begin by spray stenciling clusters of bamboo stalks all over the wall, constantly changing between brown and beige, and turning the stencil over or upside down to create as much variety as possible. Avoid anything that looks like a repeat pattern, and keep an eye out for lines or rows appearing. Think of the wall as a whole, checking all the time to see how the shapes relate to one another. Balance is very important here.

4 Once you have stenciled the stalks, begin laying the leaves over them. Once again, arrange them in clusters, and continually turn the template over and change colors. As you work across the wall (or around the room), try to create tension in the composition by leaving random spaces to contrast with the clumps of foliage.

GUIDE FOR FREEHAND PATTERN

8

A marine theme is ideally suited to the bathroom, either for very simple, subtle decoration or to indulge your fantasies and create a rich, colorful tapestry of sea creatures. For children, bathtime becomes a treat. Adults find the lovely colors calming and relaxing.

MARINE *inspirations*

The starfish, *with its five-legged body and textured surface, is a popular motif if you are decorating in a marine theme.*

At the bottom of the sea is another landscape—of valleys and hills filled with rocks, plants, and animals. Nearer the surface live creatures of exquisite colors and shapes. The forms found on land exist in the ocean in wildly different versions. With its varied, almost surreal shapes and colors, the marine world provides a wealth of inspiration for stencilers. Through the millennia, man has interpreted the underwater world in many ways. Sea creatures have often been portrayed as monsters emerging from the unknown. Sea creatures were seen as real, yet magical, bearing a resemblance to the forms we know but strangely distorted.

The sea and the creatures inhabiting it lend themselves perfectly to a decorative interpretation. The very nature of water gives all its inhabitants a fluid, graceful form, ever-changing and in constant motion. Interpretations of the ocean and water can be seen in Chinese and Japanese art, in which just a few simple lines suggest a wave or a rippling pool.

Take inspiration from the shapes and natural patterning of the ocean and its living forms. The many plants that cover the ocean floor, particularly corals, are as diverse as those found on land. Shells often have a coil formation combined with decorative patterning. A fish has a beautiful curving shape and intricate patterning on its scales. A dolphin is one of the most graceful of all animals, with a wealth of character, which it is possible to suggest in a stencil.

Spiky fish, seaweed, crabs, jellyfish, anemones, starfish, and—perhaps the strangest of all—seahorses provide a range of fantastic shapes, which lend themselves to different arrangements and forms of decoration. For example, the bold starfish shape works well as a simple treatment applied in a repeat pattern to a window shade or shower screen using bright colors. The decorative surfaces of shells provide patterns in themselves, and could be used to create a wonderfully ornate border.

Sea creatures can be simplified to create motifs for linking border patterns and simple repeats. For example, use the curving form of a fish to stencil a gently undulating border along a wall. The fluid nature of underwater plants and fish, when applied in either linear or geometric repeats, creates a soft, rhythmic pattern that works equally well on a flat surface such as a wall or tiles or on a curved surface like a freestanding bath.

The striking contrasts *of blue and yellow or orange and black on these striped fish are inspiring for both color and shape.*

A vast array of strange and
*unusual shapes and forms can be
found in shells from the sea.*

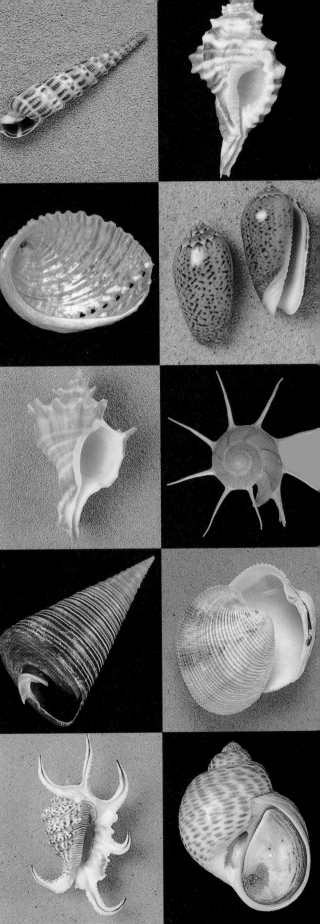

Other bathroom surfaces suitable for stenciling include floorboards and cork flooring (both of which should be sealed afterwards) and a plywood backsplash mounted on the wall behind the bath (which also needs to be sealed to protect it from splashes). Smaller expanses are also suitable, such as the medicine cabinet, sink or vanity skirt, cupboard doors, shelving units, plant pots, wastebasket, and soap dish. Even the basin and toilet could be stenciled (using ceramic paints). Three stencils feature in this section—a fish, a seahorse, and a shell—in different configurations, on a bath surround, a mirror frame, a container, and tiles. You could even stencil onto glass to create a translucent ocean view through your window. Or, if you like to lie back in the bath, create a water world on the ceiling, combining a number of different elements for a more pictorial interpretation.

The colors of the sea go well beyond "sea green." The vast range of watery blues, the vivid turquoises, the deep blues, and the pale blue-greens produced by the sun hitting the surface of the water all provide an endless source for decorative schemes. They can be used individually or combined harmoniously. Blues and greens provide the perfect background for a bathroom, as they are soothing, relaxing colors. When combined with white they have a clean, crisp feel, while the almost unworldly fluorescent reds, yellows, pinks, and other hues of the plants and fish are the perfect contrast.

This ceramic planter
*uses a stylized seahorse
motif and mosaic-effect
style, which are perfect for
a bathroom.*

MARINE COMBINATIONS

The motifs for the bathroom can be used in a wide variety of ways. You can use them on their own as a centerpiece or repeat them to make a pattern. The curving fish can be used to link other motifs or repeated to create undulating borders or more formal grids. The rigid lines of the seahorse provide a fine contrast to the curves of the fish and the almost circular shell. You can continue the aquatic theme in your color scheme by choosing watery shades of blue and green, and coral pinks, iridescent oranges, and brilliant reds.

STENCILS

Shell

Seahorse

Fish

Repeating the fish and shells in mirror image creates an attractive square that can be used on its own or stenciled randomly on fabric.

The curving forms of the fish and the upright seahorse motifs create an attractive, undulating frame.

Wall border
To adapt the square design, above, for a border design on wood paneling, the spacing can be increased so that each motif fits on one plank of wood.

Orange seahorses stenciled on a blue background create a bold, star-shaped design; the fish and shells are made to recede into the background by stenciling them in green.

The use of two colors for the seahorse adds extra interest to this formal repeat pattern.

The fluid shape of the fish creates an undulating pattern even though the motifs are on a strict diagonal grid.

Shower curtain
It is possible to stencil on the outer cloth layer of a lined shower curtain with fabric paints, but you cannot get a permanent result on a plastic curtain.

Wall cupboard
The fluid fish pattern, above left, has been taken across the joins of the door and its frame to give a lively, decorative effect.

This group of motifs can be used alone as an emblem or in a small, dotted repeat.

OCEAN WAVE BATHTUB

You'll feel as though you are bathing in the depths of the ocean with this aquatic surround for your bathtub. Blue, green and scumbled white paint, are the background for a freehand pattern of sea creatures. We used an old rolltop bathtub, but a paneled-in bathtub would be just as effective.

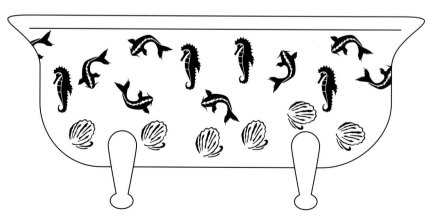

YOU WILL NEED

Rolltop or paneled-in bathtub

Enamel paints: dark blue, dark green, white, gold

2in (50mm) flat brush

Pencil

Paper

Masking tape

Stencil brush

Polyurethane yacht varnish

Varnishing brush

STENCILS

Shell

Seahorse

Fish

SUGGESTED FREEHAND PATTERN

1 Prepare the surface (see Basic Techniques) and then apply three coats of the dark blue enamel paint using the flat brush. Leave to dry after each coat.

2 While the paint is still wet, stipple in some dark green paint to give a mottled color, just as you would see in real waves. When this paint is dry, scumble a little white paint over the top, in an irregular pattern, to create the impression of wave crests.

3 Plan your design on paper to account for the shape of your bathtub or bath panel. Position clusters of shell motifs around the bottom. Vary the direction of the shells, do not let them form lines or patterns.

4 In the top half of the picture, position the seahorses and fish, which will also be stenciled. Use the curved shape of the fish to create a visual rhythm, punctuated by the vertical shapes of the seahorses. Experiment with all the shapes until you have a composition with which you are happy.

5 Now stencil the shells, seahorses, and fish in gold in the positions shown on your sketch. To protect the surface, apply two coats of varnish.

SEA CREATURES TILES

A bathroom is the perfect place for an aquatic theme. Give plain white 6in (150mm) tiles a turquoise glaze and stencil onto them sea creatures swimming in the deep, blue sea. Alternatively, you might wish to stencil the motifs straight onto tiles of any color. It is essential to use ceramic paint, or the paint will quickly wear off.

YOU WILL NEED

White tiles (in position)

Ceramic paint: turquoise

Masking tape

Stencil brush

Ruler

STENCILS

Seahorse   Shell   Fish

POSITIONAL GUIDES

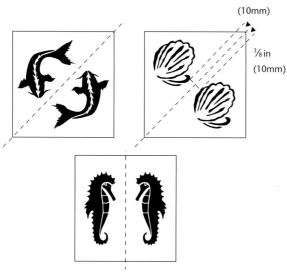

³⁄₈ in (10mm)

³⁄₈ in (10mm)

1 Use the stencil brush in a stabbing motion to stipple the turquoise paint very thinly across the tiles. You can add definition to the tile shape by painting the edges a bit more thickly. Leave to dry.

2 Hold a ruler vertically down the center of the tile and center the seahorse motif within the left half of the tile; tape in place and stencil using the turquoise paint. Turn the stencil over to create a mirror image, making sure the paint on it is dry. Check the two motifs are level, and stencil.

3 For the shells, place the ruler diagonally, from top right to bottom left, then place the stencil so the right-hand shell is about ³⁄₈in (10mm) below the diagonal. At the same time, line the stencil up with the lower edge of the tile. Tape in position and stencil in turquiose paint, then, without turning the stencil over, position it the same distance above the diagonal and lined up with the upper edge; stencil.

4 For the fish, place the ruler diagonally across the tile, from top left to bottom right. Line up the nose of the right-hand fish with the edge of the ruler on the diagonal; the lower part of the tail should be ¹⁄₂in (13mm) away from the ruler. Stencil in turquoise. Using the same side of the stencil, turn it around so the fish are nose to tail. Position as before but in reverse, and stencil.

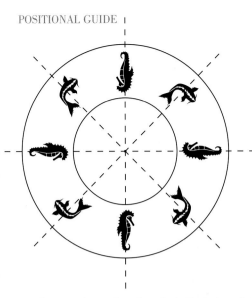

CIRCULAR MIRROR FRAME

This circular mirror frame combines the curved, darting fish motif with the more static seahorse, to add a new twist, literally, to the conventional linear border. The fluid, undulating rhythm is more suitable for a watery theme than either a linear or a geometric border would be.

1 Prepare the surface (see Basic Techniques). Using the flat brush, paint the frame with two coats of white latex paint. When it is dry, stipple the turquoise paint very thinly across it with the stencil brush.

2 Place the yardstick across the mirror, through the center. Pencil lines where it crosses the frame. Repeat for a line at right angles to this one, then two more in between those so that the frame is divided into eight equal segments.

3 Position the seahorse stencil on one of these lines so that the line cuts through the center of the seahorse. Use the yardstick to center the motif between the inner and outer edges of the frame. Stencil in turquoise paint.

4 Reposition the same stencil on the opposite side, centered on the line again, and facing in the same direction as before. Stencil in turquoise paint. Repeat on the lines halfway between these.

5 Place the fish on one of the remaining lines, adjust the position until it looks right, and mark the positions of the tail and nose. Measure how far these two points are from the edge, and mark the same distances on the remaining lines. Using turquoise paint, stencil fish at each of these positions.

6 When the paint is dry, erase the pencil lines and apply a coat of varnish to protect against the inevitable splashes and finger marks in the bathroom.

YOU WILL NEED

Round wooden mirror frame

Latex paint: white

2in (50mm) flat brush

Stencil paint: turquoise

Stencil brush

Yardstick

Pencil

Masking tape

Eraser

Satin acrylic varnish

Varnishing brush

STENCILS

Fish

Seahorse

FISHY CONTAINER

Add a marine touch to your bathroom by decorating practical storage containers with this fish motif. You can use blue and white to create a crisp, nautical look, or a palette of bright oranges, shimmering pinks, and brilliant reds to echo the colors of a tropical aquarium. We created an undulating border to mirror the curved lip of the container.

YOU WILL NEED

Readymade container

Primer

Latex paint: white

Pencil

Ruler (or tape measure for a round container)

Masking tape

Stencil brush

Stencil paint: turquoise

STENCIL

Fish

POSITIONAL GUIDE

1 Prepare the container by painting on a primer and three coats of white latex paint. Make sure the paint is completely dry before adding each coat.

2 Consider the shape of your container carefully and plan how best to place the fish motifs. If your container has a curved edge, you may want to emphasize the shape by arranging the fish in an undulating border, as shown here. Alternatively, you can stencil the motifs in a random pattern or in pairs.

3 With the nose facing inward, position the fish motif on the side of the container on the right, just below the top edge.

4 With a pencil, make one mark at the tip of the tail and another at the nose of the fish.

5 Remove the template and then mark the position required for the nose of the second fish, about ⅜in (10mm) to the left of the first fish.

6 Turn the stencil around (not over) and position the nose on the mark. Pivot the tail to the desired angle and mark its position.

7 Remove the stencil and check the pencil marks to make sure your design is well balanced.

8 To repeat the pattern, measure the points with a ruler (or tape measure if your container is round) and transfer the points to the desired location.

9 Finally, stencil the fish with turquoise paint.

9

Of all the rooms in the home, a child's room is probably the most enjoyable and satisfying to decorate. The real joy of it is to immerse yourself in a child's fantasy world and indulge your imagination—and your child's—without restraint.

CHILDREN'S
inspirations

Children have vivid imaginations, and the best inspiration for their rooms will usually come from them. If you work through the creative process together, ideas will evolve that you would probably never have thought of otherwise. It also makes it more likely that the child will actually like the result and will not eventually cover up your handiwork with posters. Choosing a decorative scheme that will stand the test of time and a child's rapidly changing interests is extremely difficult. With small children, the bolder and brighter the colors, the better. However, if a calmer atmosphere is needed, then try pastel tones such as the colors of ice cream: vanilla, strawberry, blueberry, and pistachio.

Much inspiration can be found in the child's favorite books and toys. Illustrations with bold shapes and simple color effects are easily adapted

Your child would be *delighted to see his or her favorite cartoon character stenciled as a frieze or border around the room.*

to stencils. Numbers and letters form bold patterns and are, at the same time, educational. Animal markings can be stenciled to create wild jungle images.

Children's toys *can provide inspiraton for stencil shapes, and your children will love seeing their favorite doll painted on a toy-chest.*

Nature offers a wealth of inspiration with varied flower and leaf shapes, and these images will not be outgrown too quickly. We have used colorful flowers for three of the projects in this chapter. With their striking shapes, the flowers look dramatic and, more importantly, are easily recognizable. The inspiration for the colors we used came from 1960s pop art, with its contrasting primary hues. The designs and colors are stimulating for a baby or toddler yet not too childish for an older child.

Various other stencils in this book, particularly the marine motifs and geometric shapes, are also suitable for children's rooms. The canvas wardrobe project in this chapter, which is decorated with just three geometric shapes—the square, heart, and five-pointed star—is a good illustration of how other designs can be adapted.

Any number of things in a child's room are potential candidates for stenciling. The projects in this chapter

Animal prints
*can be used
to create large,
wild patterns
or to decorate the
smallest of objects.*

The cartoon quality and
*bright colors of a rubber duck
are perfect for stencils.*

involve decorating a portable canvas wardrobe, a roller shade, a lampshade, and a picture frame. A canvas floorcloth could be stenciled with a game or a railway track for toy trains. Storage boxes, wastebaskets, height charts, closet doors, toy-chests, drawers, shelf edges —the list of possibilities is endless.

Make sure that all materials used are safe and washable. Acrylic paint is safe and can be wiped clean, but it is a good idea to apply a layer of flat acrylic varnish over the top for added protection.

Finally, if your child is old enough, try to involve them in the stenciling. The result may not be perfect, and you may have to simplify the design, but the child will love it all the more if they have helped with the decoration.

A lion's mane creates a
*flaming sunflower shape.
Stencil the basic shape
and then add the details
of nose and eyes by hand.*

Teddy bears will always
*be loved, so try stenciling
a friendly teddy shape on
your child's headboard.*

CHILDREN'S COMBINATIONS

Spectacular, bold designs for a child's bedroom can be created with the floral motifs and the solid heart and star shapes. You can combine the motifs in a variety of ways to create grid patterns, abstract designs, or individual emblems. Bright colors work best with these motifs and are very effective in a child's room.

STENCILS

Daisy

Marguerite

Leafy stalk

Heart

Star

Crysanthemum

Crib
Although the central motif design, left, could have been repeated across the whole of the crib, it is often more effective to use a single cluster.

To add a stylized element to a floral pattern, consider using geometric motifs too. Here, the circles help to define the group of flowers' shape.

This diamond cluster of marguerites, blazing in yellow around a more subdued daisy, can be used alone for a cushion cover or as a repeat on curtain fabric.

For a border, it is simple to alternate between one flower and another. You could also build up a more complex version with extra flowers and more colors.

Stenciling white stars on a blue background creates a stunning abstract pattern.

Laundry basket

An otherwise plain laundry basket is transformed by a band of blue stars, stenciled in the point-to-point pattern, as above right.

This clean, bright repeat was created by combining the daisy and leafy stalk motifs. The blue and green background and the white flowers give the design a fresh, crisp look.

A bright, fun pattern is created by a repeat of white daisies and deep red hearts on a colored background.

Toy-box

You can add freehand elements to any design. Here, the daisy and heart pattern, above, has been made more three-dimensional with some shading on the heart shapes.

FLOWERY PICTURE FRAME

Vibrant colors and a slightly abstract design give this double picture frame a cheerful, contemporary look that children of all ages will love. The wood background was left natural, but it could be painted if you prefer. Why not stencil a collection of frames in different colors and patterns?

SUGGESTED FREEHAND PATTERN

1 Although the flowers are stenciled randomly onto the frame, you still need to think about arrangement. Stencils do not always have to fit perfectly within the edges of the frame or other object. Placing them slightly "off" the item, or using stencils that are too wide, creates a more abstract pattern and contemporary look. Try not to think in terms of rigid patterns but more of random clusters that are balanced by the colors used.

2 Begin stenciling with the strongest colors in your design, in this case, the purple and cobalt blue, both of which are used with the daisy stencil. Occasionally, use the two colors for different petals on the same flower. Place some of the repeats farther in than others, and turn the stencils around, changing direction continually to give balance across the frame. Be careful not to create rigid lines of flowers.

3 Now begin stenciling the marguerite stencil in minty green. Don't just fill in the spaces between the flowers, actually stencil right across them.

4 Take the motif over and around the edges of the frame by wrapping the stencil around them. Secure it with masking tape to make sure that it doesn't move and that it joins up with the pattern on the front.

YOU WILL NEED

Wooden picture frame

Masking tape

Stencil paints: minty green, cobalt blue, purple, white

Stencil brush

STENCILS

Marguerite

Daisy

Plain paper lampshades provide the perfect background for vibrant colors and simple, striking images that glow

LEAFY STALK LAMPSHADE

when lit up at night. Rather than creating a very literal interpretation of the flowers that encircle the shade, we reversed the colors and stenciled green flowers and yellow foliage.

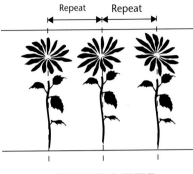

Repeat   Repeat

POSITIONAL GUIDE

1 Using the tape measure, measure around the top of the lampshade. Work out how much space you need to allow between the repeats in order for them to be spaced evenly, and using a pencil, lightly mark the positions of the repeats at the top of the shade.

2 Place the marguerite stencil on one of the marks, with the top petal pointing upward in line with the penciled mark. Tape into position; stencil in minty green.

3 Before stenciling the next flower, turn the stencil so that a different petal is point up. Carry on around the shade in this way. Avoid placing the motifs in a regimented line—the line should undulate slightly.

4 Place the leafy stalk stencil about ¾in (20mm) away from one of the flowers, and mark the position of the bottom of the stem on the shade with a small pencil dot. Measure the distance from the mark to the bottom of the shade, and mark out the repeats all the way around.

5 Position the leafy stalk stencil so that the top lines up with the flower and the bottom with the marked point. Tape it in place, and stencil in cadmium yellow.

6 Stencil the remaining leafy stalk repeats yellow, keeping the stems so that they are all pointing in the same direction.

STENCILS

Leafy stalk

Marguerite

YOU WILL NEED

Paper lampshade

Tape measure

Pencil

Masking tape

Stencil paints: minty green, cadmium yellow

Stencil brush

MULTICOLOR WARDROBE

The technique of overlaying colors and motifs adds another dimension to stenciling, and the large, flat surfaces of a canvas wardrobe provide an ideal surface for this graphic technique. The bold colors and motifs will interest a small child as well as turning a household item into an attractive feature.

YOU WILL NEED

Portable canvas wardrobe

Protective plastic sheet

Tape measure

Pencil

Yardstick

Fabric paints: magenta, cadmium yellow, purple, orange, ultramarine, green

Stencil brush

Masking tape

Iron

Overstenciling

The various elements of overstenciling can be combined in any number of ways to create the striking look of a screen print. Simple, strong motifs and colors work best so that the image is not partially lost. We only stenciled sections of the wardrobe, leaving a large border around the stenciling on each side. However, each side could be completely covered with the design for a more intense, colorful result.

STENCILS

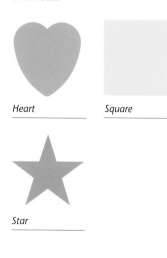

Heart

Square

Star

POSITIONAL GUIDES

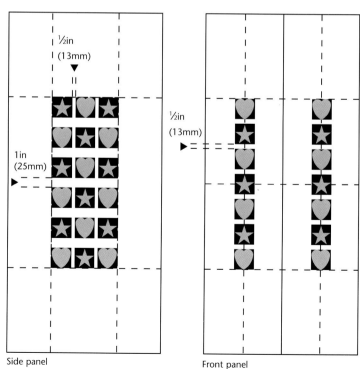

½in (13mm)

1in (25mm)

½in (13mm)

Side panel

Front panel

1 Place the wardrobe on a table protected with a plastic sheet with the front lying flat. Treating each side of the zipper as a separate panel, measure and mark the center point of each panel. Center the square stencil over this mark, and stencil in orange.

2 Leave a ½in (13mm) gap above the orange square and stencil the next square in purple, the next in yellow, and then one in magenta, leaving the same gap between each of them. Going back to the orange square, leave a ½in (13mm) gap below it and stencil a magenta square, then below this another in yellow, and another in purple. Do this on each side of the zipper.

3 When the paint is dry, you can begin over-stenciling. On the front, each motif has its own color and its own square. Center the heart stencil on a yellow square and stencil a magenta heart on top. Apply the paint sparingly, other-wise you will not see the color underneath.

4 Stencil magenta hearts on the other yellow squares, then stencil green hearts on the orange squares, yellow stars on the magenta squares, and ultramarine stars on the purple squares.

5 On the side of the wardrobe, you will want to paint several columns of squares because the panel is wider. To keep the design light, we have left more space between the squares. It also helps to leave a large border of plain canvas. This grid has six squares with 1in (25mm) gaps in each column and ½in (13mm) gaps between the three columns. If you wish, stencil the squares of color and then the motifs at random rather than in a particular order, but avoid placing the same colors or motifs next to one another.

6 Fix the paints with an iron following the manufacturer's instructions.

DAISY ROLLER SHADE

Stenciling a roller shade not only livens up the shade, but also allows you to coordinate your window with the rest of the room. It is ideal for children's rooms, as you can choose anything from feminine flowers to riotous primary colors.

1 Lay the shade out on a flat surface, fully extended. The design is based on a square grid. Don't draw the grid on the shade, as it would be difficult to rub off. Instead, just mark a pencil point for each motif, starting with the first row of flowers at the bottom.

2 Measuring up from the first row, mark the next row of flowers (*not* the hearts), working your way up to the top of the shade. Draw a pencil registration line across the center of each of the flower stencils.

3 Place the yardstick with its upper edge along the first row of points and its left-hand end at the left-hand point. Position the daisy stencil with the registration line aligned with the edge of the ruler.

4 Tape down the corners of the stencil, and then slide the yardstick out. Stencil a powder blue daisy. Using the other flower stencil, apply a magenta chrysanthemum at the next point in the row. Continue in this way, alternating stencils and colors all over the shade. Stencil a yellow circle motif in the center of every flower.

5 Adding heart and square motifs gives you a checker-board pattern. Lay the rulers diagonally between the centers of two pairs of flowers and mark the point where they cross. Center the square by eye over this point and stencil in yellow. Stencil a pink heart over the top. Repeat as shown on the grid.

6 Fix the fabric paints by ironing according to the manufacturer's instructions.

YOU WILL NEED

Plain roller shade

Sheet of plastic to protect work surface

Yardstick

Pencil

Masking tape

Fabric paints: powder blue, pink, magenta, yellow

Stencil brush

Iron

POSITIONAL GUIDE

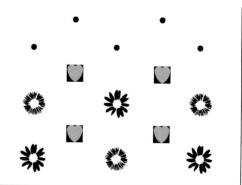

STENCILS

| Heart | Square | Circle | Daisy | Chrysanthemum |

10

There is no need to limit stenciling to the inside of the home. People relax and entertain out of doors, too, so here is another opportunity to adorn your surroundings. Organic forms are the best source of inspiration, and they create a special harmony when set against nature's own backdrop.

GARDEN
inspirations

Like a child's room, the garden is a canvas on which your imagination can run riot. Unlike the inside of the house, it is not governed by architectural restraints. Colors, designs, and patterns that would be too much in the interior sit happily next to nature's rich tapestry.

Nature provides the ultimate inspiration for the decorative artist, so where better to find ideas for designs than, literally, in your own backyard? Look at its structures and plants, and the forms of the flowers and leaves, and then create your own personal, individual designs.

The stencils featured in this section are three flowers—daisy, marguerite, and chrysanthemum—and the sprig, stalk, leafy stalk, and natural leaf. Other stencils in the book would also be suitable, particularly the classical leaf, large curl and simple curl, berries, bamboo leaf and stalk, and classical and Indian leaf sprays.

A deep border
in a cottage garden is filled with an array of colorful flowers.

And, of course, there is no need to restrict yourself to organic forms; stylized or abstract motifs can look stunning in a garden. Large, bold designs are well suited to the larger scale of nature, but small repeat patterns can also look good.

The simple shape *of an aster can easily be made into a stencil for all-year flowers and color.*

Designing your own stencils from nature is more difficult than basing them on an illustration, which has already been reduced from three dimensions to two. It's a good idea to choose a relatively simple plant, or you could find a picture of the plant and then trace that. Once you have a drawing, you need to simplify it, omitting superfluous parts and emphasizing the important ones. Decide where to put the "bridges," which hold the stencil together. They can be straight or curved, short or long, depending on the shape, and should follow the lines of the design without interfering with it.

The projects in this section involve stenciling a garden table and canvas director's chair, a terra-cotta plant pot, and, for fun, a sun hat. Wooden garden

benches and Adirondack chairs would also be easy to stencil, and so would wooden planters. Tired old deckchairs and seat cushions could be re-covered with brightly stenciled fabrics, and a plain garden umbrella could be jazzed up with a fun design.

Non-portable items can come under the stencil brush, too. Exterior shutters and window boxes, even shed doors and painted brick walls are possibilities. Why not transform your walls and fences with vivid colors and patterns? Bear in mind that any items that will be exposed to weather should ideally be painted with alkyd rather than water-based paints, and should be well sealed with a good varnish such as yacht varnish.

Stenciled color and pattern can be used to enhance or even create features of particular interest. Draw attention to an ornamental pond with a mosaic effect created by stenciling different-colored squares on drab stone paving. Enliven an ugly wall or concrete barbecue by stenciling a climbing vine over it.

As in a room, backyard decoration can be themed. For a nautical theme, install sail-like canopies stenciled with boating motifs over a wooden deck. If your lawn gets too much for you, replace it with pebbles; add large pieces of driftwood, along with deckchairs and windbreaks stenciled with seaside images such as waves and shells. Or, if you have a roof terrace in a city, play up the urban landscape by stenciling skyscrapers on painted walls.

The best source of color inspiration for garden decoration will come from the natural colorings found in the garden itself. Often, colors one would never combine in the home look wonderful when juxtaposed in nature. You can work in harmony using oranges and reds on your plant pots to echo the fiery tones of geraniums, dahlias, and marigolds, or use complementary mauves and blues to create contrast.

Nature provides *us with striking contrasts of colors and forms.*

Color can be used to unify different
floral motifs. Blue and white decoration has a timeless appeal.

GARDEN COMBINATIONS

You can use the floral and leaf motifs in a variety of combinations to create stencil designs suitable for a garden. The three flowers can be combined with the leaf spray and sprig motifs to create an almost endless array of patterns. Use the various leaves and stalks to create borders of creeping vines, or simply combine the flowers on their own to make stunning repeat patterns. Stenciling items for use in a garden or balcony gives you an excellent chance to experiment with color combinations that you would not usually choose for an interior.

STENCILS

Daisy

Marguerite

Chrysanthemum

Natural leaf

Stalk

Leafy stalk

The sprig, circle, and daisy motifs are combined to create a light, summery design that works as a repeat or border.

Garden basket

What could be more pleasant than filling a flower-covered garden basket with fresh-cut flowers? It will also look good out of season.

The sprig motifs link the marguerites in the four corners. The pattern is reinforced by using strong colors for both the motifs.

The bright red chrysanthemums in this diagonal repeat pattern are well balanced by the bright green stalk motifs.

Here the group of sprig and circle motifs in the center balances the marguerite motifs used in the corners, and emphasizes the underlying diagonal grid.

Parasol

The lattice effect created by extending the sprig and daisy pattern, left, is perfect for covering relatively large surfaces.

The curving sprig draws the eye toward the central daisy. When the pattern is repeated, the sprigs form an undulating vine across the design.

Watering can

The diagonal stalk pattern, below right, works well when repeated around a watering can. Fill any awkward spaces with extra stalk motifs.

With a bright daisy as its central focus, this design is ideal for a cushion cover. It can also be repeated to make a striking fabric pattern.

SCATTERED LEAF TABLETOP

Brighten up plain and functional garden furniture with stenciled motifs. This tabletop has been decorated with

leaves in a random pattern, as though they had just fallen from the trees. This design uses the subtle greens and yellows of nature, but for an alternative, brighter color scheme you could incorporate autumnal reds, oranges, and purples.

YOU WILL NEED

Wooden or metal picnic table

Exterior paints, such as enamel or spray paints (for a metal table), or oil-based eggshell (for a wooden table): pale yellow, cadmium yellow, pale green, leaf green, olive green

2in (50mm) decorator's brush

Masking tape

Stencil brush

Yacht varnish or polyurethane varnish

Varnishing brush

STENCILS

Leafy stalk

Stalk

SUGGESTED FREEHAND PATTERN

1 Prepare the surface for painting (see Basic Techniques) and then paint the whole table with at least two coats of pale yellow. Mask off the lower part of the stem of the stalk stencil with masking tape, and the lower stem and leaf of the leafy stalk stencil, as these portions will not be used.

2 Place the leafy stalk stencil on the table at random and stencil it in leaf green or olive green. Use the brush more heavily in the center to darken this area. Highlight around the edges with pale green and use cadmium yellow on the tips. Blend the edges of the colors into each other without mixing them together completely. This shading and highlighting will create a more realistic effect than just using a single color.

3 Stencil the remaining leaves with one stencil or the other at random, using all four colors but varying the effects so that some are darker, some more yellow, and so on. Turn the stencils so that they face in different directions.

4 Fill in the spaces with individual leaves, again varying the color and direction. Don't cram the tabletop too full of leaves—the design should look light and delicate.

5 To make the table more weather-resistant, apply three coats of yacht or polyurethane varnish, using the varnishing brush. Let it dry completely between each coat.

DIRECTOR'S CHAIR

Director's chairs are modern classics and the flat, rectangular canvas back and seat are ideal for stenciling. Take inspiration from the colorful textile designs of the 1950s, and give a formal grid pattern a fun twist. Use bold motifs and overstencil it in a different color as if the pattern has been slightly misprinted.

YOU WILL NEED

Director's chair

Sheet of plastic to protect work surface

Tailor's chalk

Yardstick

Pencil

Fabric paints: yellow, orange

Stencil brush

Iron

STENCILS

Daisy

Chrysanthemum

Marguerite

POSITIONAL GUIDES

Back

Seat

1 Measure the back and seat of the chair, and work out your spacing. You can usually remove the canvas pieces from the chair, and it is easier to decorate them if you lay them flat on a table, protected with a sheet of plastic. Using tailor's chalk and a yardstick, draw your grid on the canvas pieces.

2 On each stencil, draw registration lines across the visual center of each flower. Place a stencil on the back panel and line up the registration lines with the grid. Stencil in the appropriate color (we used orange for the daisy and yellow for the chrysanthemum).

3 For the seat panel, stencil a daisy in orange at the central point of the grid, and at two of the corners. Next stencil chrysanthemums in yellow along the next diagonal row (see grid) and finally orange marguerites in the two remaining corners.

4 When the paint is dry, you can start overstenciling. Place the daisy stencil on an already stenciled daisy, twisting it very slightly so that the registration lines don't quite meet. Stencil in yellow for the orange flowers, and orange for the yellow flowers. Apply the paint quite thinly so the underneath layer still shows through, creating a third color.

5 Fix the fabric paints by ironing, according to the manufacturer's instructions.

LEAFY PLANT POT

Make your plant pots as interesting as the plants in them, and decorate them with colorful motifs. The design could be stenciled straight onto the terra-cotta, or you could do as we have done and paint the pot first with a background color in order to create a greater contrast.

1 If desired, paint the pot with at least two coats of lime green, using the flat brush.

2 Measure around the rim of the pot with the tape measure, and work out the spacing of the sprig motifs, marking the positions on the rim.

3 Stencil orange sprigs at these marks, centering them between the top and bottom edges of the rim. (Be sure to tape the stencil firmly in place on the curved surface.) Stencil more heavily in some spots than others, to create lighter and darker areas.

4 Place the leafy stalk stencil on the pot and decide what height and angle look best. Mark the highest and lowest points (the point of the top leaf and the tip of the stem) on the pot, then remove the stencil.

5 Measure how far the upper point is from the bottom of the rim, and mark this distance several times around the pot. Do the same for the distance the lower point is from the base. Run masking tape around the pot so that the bottom edge of the tape is even with the upper marks. Run another strip around the pot so that its top edge is even with the lower marks. Measure around the lower tape and work out the spacing of the motifs (see Basic Techniques), and mark the positions on the tape.

6 Place the leafy stalk stencil so that the highest and lowest points are on the inner edges of the two lines of tape and on the positions marked. Stencil in orange, creating lighter and darker areas (see step 3). Remove the tape. Apply two or three coats of varnish, letting each coat dry before applying the next, if the pot will be left outside.

YOU WILL NEED

Terra-cotta plant pot

Stencil paints: lime green, orange

2in (50mm) flat brush

Tape measure

Pencil

Masking tape

Stencil brush

Polyurethane varnish (optional)

Varnishing brush (optional)

STENCILS

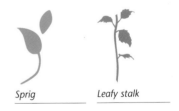

Sprig   Leafy stalk

POSITIONAL GUIDES

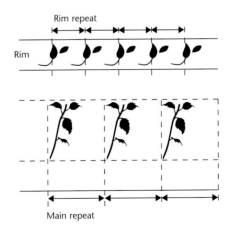

MARGUERITE SUN HAT

Clothes and accessories can be stenciled just as you would a wall or table. With a rigid piece, such as a hat, both structured and fluid designs work well. Because a sun hat is fun and frivolous, we have scattered summery flowers over the hat at random, creating a colorful accessory that is both practical and decorative.

SUGGESTED FREEHAND PATTERN

YOU WILL NEED

Straw sun hat

Masking tape

Sheet of plastic, to protect rest of hat

Spray paints: russet, leaf green

STENCILS

Marguerite

Natural leaf

1 Tape the marguerite stencil to the brim of the hat and cover the rest of it with the plastic sheet.

2 Working in a well-ventilated area, preferably outdoors hold the can of russet paint upright about 3–6in (75–150mm) from the hat, and apply a fine spray through the stencil. Spray paints are best to use for this, as it is very difficult to get into the nooks and crannies of the straw weave with a paintbrush.

3 Stencil more russet flowers and some leaf-green leaves around the hat, grouping them in clusters and leaving some areas clear. Vary the direction of the stencils, turning them over and around to avoid obvious repetition. Place some slightly off the hat, for a lively, modern look. Do not try to cover the whole hat with flowers and leaves—just create a fairly balanced look and try to give the impression that the flowers have fallen into small groups.

Once you have made some of the projects in the previous section, you will start to think about designing your own stencils. The six projects here will get you started but you can also use personal motifs to suit your home and delight your friends.

MAKE YOUR
own stencils

Elephant Frieze

Stencil this simple linear pattern onto long strips of brown wrapping paper, then stick it on the wall for a child's birthday party. Children may like it so much that they won't let you take it down! The colors of the elephants were inspired by elephants used in Indian religious festivals, which are adorned with lavish pigments and fabrics.

YOU WILL NEED

Tracing paper (if using stencil card)

Pencil and ruler

Fiber-tip pen (if using Mylar)

Oiled manila stencil card or Mylar

Rubber cutting mat

Mat knife or craft knife

Brown wrapping paper

Acrylic paints: cerulean blue, pink, gold

Stencil brush

1 If you are using oiled manila stencil card, trace the elephant outline from your drawing, and transfer it to the card. If you are using clear Mylar, draw the elephant straight onto it.

2 Place the stencil on a cutting mat. Allow at least 2in (50mm) all around the motif, for strength and to prevent smudges.

3 Cut around the outer edges of the stencil with a craft knife. Then cut out the elephant-shaped window. Make sure there are no ragged edges on the elephant outline.

4 Center the elephant motif vertically on the strip of paper. Tape the stencil in position and stencil in blue. Stencil the next one in pink, then continue along the line, alternating colors.

5 Over each stenciled motif, stencil a light coating of gold paint.

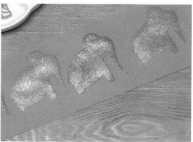

6 By stenciling only lightly in gold, the pink and blue base colors show through, creating a striking decorative effect.

Frosty T-shirt

The design on this T-shirt comes from the type of symbols found on most computers. Many generic symbols, such as arrows and weather symbols can be taken from such modern sources. Graphic images surround us every day, ranging from traffic signs to company logos, and they offer a rich choice of contemporary motifs suitable for stenciling.

YOU WILL NEED

T-shirt

Computer printout of "frost" symbol

Ruler

Pencil (if using stencil card)

Tracing paper (if using stencil card)

Fiber-tip pen (if using Mylar)

Oiled manila stencil card or Mylar

Cutting mat

Craft knife or mat knife

Masking tape

Fabric paints: cerulean blue, white

Stencil brush

Iron

1 From your printout enlarge your chosen symbol on a photocopier. If you are using stencil card, trace the symbol from the printout onto tracing paper using a ruler and a pencil.

2 Using the ruler, either transfer the symbol to stencil card with a pencil, or trace it from the printout straight onto clear Mylar.

3 Still using the ruler, place the stencil on the cutting mat and cut out the image with a mat knife or craft knife.

4 Plan where to position the motifs, then tape the stencil in place. Use the brush to stencil in white first, then stipple the blue lightly over the top.

5 Repeat for the remaining motifs. Fix the paints with an iron, following the manufacturer's directions.

Leaf Cards and Gift Wrap

Greeting cards and gift-wrapping paper you have stenciled yourself are fun to give and a delight to receive. We used heavy watercolor paper for the greeting cards, tearing rather than cutting the edges, and brown wrapping paper for the gift wrap.

Whether you live in a rural or urban environment, it is possible to find wind-blown leaves and twigs. To create an image that could be the basis of a stencil design, you can either make direct rubbings or trace from a photocopy, allowing you to adjust the size. Some adaptation may be necessary to make the design practical.

YOU WILL NEED

Wind-blown leaves

Thin paper

Pencil

Tracing paper (if using stencil card)

Oiled manila stencil card or Mylar

Fiber-tip pen (if using Mylar)

Cutting mat

Craft knife or mat knife

Masking tape

Stencil brush

Acrylic paint: olive green

Low-tack spray glue

Synthetic sponge

Heavy watercolor paper torn to twice the size of your finished card and folded in half

Greeting Cards

1 Place a piece of thin paper over a leaf and rub a soft pencil over it. The outline and veins will appear. If you will be using stencil card, trace the shape onto tracing paper first.

2 The vein pattern is stenciled in a different color from the leaf itself, so you need separate stencils. Trace the leaf outline onto stencil card, or draw it directly onto Mylar with a fiber-tip pen.

3 Transfer the vein pattern onto a separate piece of card or Mylar.

4 Using a cutting mat and craft knife, cut out the leaf stencil and the vein-shaped stencil. Do not discard the cut-out shape from the leaf stencil.

5 Tape the leaf stencil onto a card and tape the card to your work surface. Stencil in olive green with a stencil brush.

6 With low-tack spray glue, stick the cut-out center from the leaf stencil to the front of another card. Use the sponge to dab olive green paint around it, leaving a rough, uneven margin.

7 When the paint is dry, position the vein stencil in the blank leaf space. Tape down and stencil in olive green using the brush.

8 The two designs complement each other, with the colors, shapes, and materials making them a perfect set.

YOU WILL NEED

Wind-blown leaves and twig

Pencil

Tracing paper (if using stencil card)

Oiled manila stencil card or Mylar

Fiber-tip pen (if using Mylar)

Cutting mat

Craft knife or mat knife

Masking tape

Brown wrapping paper

Stencil brush

Acrylic paints: duck egg blue, burnt umber

Paper

Gift Wrap

1 Choose a leaf. Enlarge it on a photocopier to the size you want.

2 If you will be using stencil card, make a tracing of the photocopied image on tracing paper first.

3 Either transfer the traced outline onto the stencil card or draw it directly onto Mylar.

4 Using a cutting mat and a craft knife, cut out the stencil.

5 Tape the stencil in place anywhere on the brown paper, and use the stencil brush to stencil in duck egg blue. Repeat randomly over the paper.

6 Draw a twig shape on some paper. You will get a more realistic result if you copy a real twig.

7 Trace the twig shape onto stencil card, or draw it onto Mylar. Using a cutting mat and a craft knife, cut it out.

8 Place the twig stencil across a stenciled leaf and stencil in burnt umber, using the brush.

9 Stencil more twigs at random.

Bulletin Board

The New York skyline at sunset is stenciled along the bottom of this bulletin board, leaving plenty of room for display yet making the board look good even when it is empty. The skyline consists of a repeat of the Chrysler Building and the Seagram Building, both unmistakable sights in the city.

YOU WILL NEED

Paper

Fiber-tip pen

Ruler

Tracing paper (if using stencil card)

Pencil (if using stencil card)

Oiled manila stencil card or Mylar

Cutting mat

Ruler

Craft knife or mat knife

Cork bulletin board

Latex paint: white

1in (25mm) flat brush

Acrylic paints: cadmium yellow, cadmium red

Masking tape

1 Using a fiber-tip pen, make a simplified sketch of the two buildings, using photographs or postcards as your reference.

2 Either trace the sketch onto stencil card, or trace it directly onto clear Mylar using a fiber-tip pen.

3 Place the stencil on a cutting mat and, using a ruler and craft knife, cut out the images.

4 To create a clean, crisp background, paint the board with white latex using the flat brush.

5 While the white latex is still wet, paint yellow acrylic over it, starting at the top and gradually fading the yellow out and blending it into the white.

6 Position the building motif in the bottom corner of the board. Use the stencil brush to apply red acrylic at the bottom and blend it into yellow toward the top.

7 Move the stencil along, leaving a space, and then repeat the process until the bottom of the bulletin board is filled.

Musical Notes Napkins

Musical notes can be highly decorative, and these stenciled paper napkins are truly noteworthy! You could make them specially for a party or a picnic to please a musical friend.

YOU WILL NEED

Ruler

Fiber-tip pen

Paper

Tracing paper (if using stencil card)

Pencil (if using stencil card)

Oiled manila stencil card or Mylar

Cutting mat

Craft knife or mat knife

Paper napkins

Acrylic paints: black, gold

1 Use a ruler and fiber-tip pen to draw the notes on paper.

2 Either trace the notes onto the stencil card, or draw them straight onto a sheet of Mylar. Cut them out, using a ruler and craft knife.

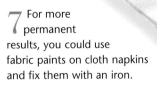

3 Position the stencil on the napkin and stencil in black. Repeat at random. Then stencil more notes in gold, overlapping the black ones.

4 Don't stencil the notes too close together—they should be loosely scattered to give a light design.

7 For more permanent results, you could use fabric paints on cloth napkins and fix them with an iron.

INDEX

CREDITS

Quarto would like to thank and acknowledge the sources given below for pictures reproduced on the following pages:

Clark/Clinch: 40r, 41 l & r, 51 br; Penny Cobb: 51 t; e. t. archive: 30 l, 61 b, 71 t & b; Garden Picture Library/John Glover: 110 l; Image Bank: 40 l; Anna Watson: 81 tl.

Key   t = top l = left r = right b = bottom

All other pictures are the copyright of Quarto

Quarto would like to thank C. P. Hart for the loan of the bathtub featured on pages 94-95.
C. P. Hart, Newnham Terrace, Hercules Road, London SE1 7DR.